Strategic Planning
In College Libraries

CLIP Note # 43

Compiled by

Eleonora Dubicki
Associate Librarian
Monmouth University
West Long Branch, New Jersey

College Library Information Packet Committee
College Libraries Section
Association of College and Research Libraries
A Division of the American Library Association

The paper used in this publication meets the minimum requirements of the American National Standard for Information Sciences-Permanence of Paper for Printed Library Materials, ANSI Z39.48-1992.

Library of Congress Cataloging-in-Publication Data

Strategic planning in college libraries / compiled by Eleonora Dubicki.
    p. cm. -- (CLIP note ; #43)
  Includes bibliographical references and index.
  ISBN 978-0-8389-8588-5 (pbk. : alk. paper) 1. Academic libraries--United States--Planning. 2. Strategic planning--United States. 3. Library surveys--United States. I. Dubicki, Eleonora.
  Z675.U5S819 2011
  027.70973--dc23
                2011017431

Printed in the United States of America.

15 14 13 12 11   5 4 3 2 1

Cover design by Jim Lange Design

TABLE OF CONTENTS

Documents (6–10 Pages):

Documents (10+ Pages):

v

CLIP NOTES COMMITTEE MEMBERS

Gillian S. Gremmels, Chair
E.H. Little Library
Davidson College
Davidson, North Carolina

Jennie E. Callas, Lead Editor
McGraw-Page Library
Randolph-Macon College
Ashland, Virginia

Jane P. Currie
Cudahy Library
Loyola University Chicago
Chicago, Illinois

Melinda K. Dermody
Syracuse University
Syracuse, New York

Nancy E. Frazier
Bucknell University
Lewisburg, Pennsylvania

Elizabeth Hoppe
Schaffer Library
Union College
Schenectady, New York

Erin T. Smith
McGill Library
Westminster College
New Wilmington, Pennsylvania

Doris Ann Sweet
Assumption College Library
Worcester, Massachusetts

Nancy J. Weiner
David and Lorraine Cheng Library
William Paterson University
Wayne, New Jersey

ACKNOWLEDGEMENTS

The compiler would like to especially thank Jennie Callas for her assistance as the editor for this publication.

INTRODUCTION

OBJECTIVE

The College Library Information Packet (CLIP) Notes publishing program, under the auspices of the College Libraries Section of the Association of College and Research Libraries (ACRL), provides "college and small university libraries with state-of-the-art reviews and current documentation on library practices and procedures of relevance to them" (Morein 1985). The focus of this CLIP Note is strategic planning in college libraries.

Strategic planning is the process of identifying an organization's goals and objectives for the future. Strategic planning was originally used in the military, but during the 1960's and 1970's it became increasingly popular as a management tool for businesses. More recently, strategic planning has been embraced by the public sector, including higher education. As academic institutions endeavor to attract new students, many have developed strategic plans to guide them in achieving enrollment and curricular goals. Many academic libraries have responded with their own strategic plans that support institutional goals and chart a roadmap for how libraries will meet their users' needs in the future.

BACKGROUND

Academic libraries have experienced dramatic changes during the last few decades due to the transformation of the information environment. With the growth of the Internet and a strong shift to electronic formats, patrons are using many library resources and services differently than they did in the past. Libraries must be prepared to successfully meet the demands of digital users, as well as those using print library resources. Furthermore, as colleges and universities are affected by cuts in state and federal funding, colleges are closely scrutinizing their budgets, including allocations for libraries. As a result, strategic planning has become a vital component of preparing for the future success of academic libraries.

A review of library literature revealed that more than 20 years ago, Oberembt (1988) surveyed academic libraries for a CLIP Note on Annual Reports and found that the top-rated reasons for their value were: "1. to publicize library achievements; 2. to explain future needs; 3. to justify continued financial support." More recently, Sauer (2006) found that annual reports provide librarians with a picture for long-term development and strategic planning.

Strategic planning focuses on the library's future by defining goals and objectives and the sequence of steps or actions to achieve those goals. The strategic planning process is based on analysis: where are we right now, where do we want to be, and how we can get there? In an academic library, a strategic plan can develop a course of action for the future as the library endeavors to meet the needs of a new generation of students and faculty. Brown and Blake Gonzalez (2007) completed a review of the origins of strategic planning, various models used by academic libraries and the positive and negative impacts strategic planning can have on libraries. Clement (1995) found that strategic planning in research libraries "appears to be far and away the most common mode of planning and with few exceptions has been deemed successful by library and university administrators." Accordingly, the strategic plan has become a vital tool for setting goals and objectives to guide library employees, as well as a tool for library advocacy on campus.

Dougherty (2002) urges libraries to embrace change in our profession, but advocates that libraries should utilize strategic planning to "plan for change, not merely react to it." Pacios (2004) finds that libraries use strategic planning to improve and enhance precious information resources and library services in very focused ways in order to achieve identified goals for the benefit of students and faculty.

Birdsall discusses strategic planning in the context of institution-wide planning cycles. He proposes that "by acknowledging the political basis of decision making in organizations, libraries can build coalitions and alliances in their institutions at large." Consequently, mission and goals align with those of the university. Birdsall also recommends involving multiple groups on campus in the strategic planning process, thereby creating broader support for libraries across the institution. Butler and Davis (1992) also endorse this approach of engaging other campus units in strategic planning. Similarly, Franklin (2009) focuses on aligning library strategies to university academic plans.

Several articles in the literature provide insights into how individual libraries conducted the strategic planning process. Schulz (1998) discusses the Maryville University Library's use of an environmental assessment (SWOT analysis) to identify strengths and weakness, as well as build on opportunities and minimize threats. Miller (2009) describes how Eastern Washington University Libraries met with faculty members to draft a vision for the role of the libraries and how the process impacted library planning.

A number of recent articles focus on using strategic planning documents to create awareness on campus regarding the changing role of the library within the university setting, particularly in the areas of information literacy and delivery of services. Decker and Hoppner (2006) contend that while most customers have a traditional understanding of libraries and their services, few customers are aware of the financial costs of building state-of-the-art information sources that seamlessly connect users to electronic materials. Ryan (2003) shows how strategic planning can be adapted for a library's website development and management. Little and Huten (2006) discuss how to use strategic planning to promote information literacy among academic faculty.

Rigg's 1984 and Mathew's 2005 publications are two books which have been produced on strategic planning for libraries, providing good overviews of the planning process. As part of the Public Library Association Results series, Nelson (2008) published a book on the planning process and a companion volume that covers implementation of strategic plans. While targeted at public libraries, academic libraries can adapt many elements from these books.

The purpose of this study was to gather information on how academic libraries develop strategic plans and to collect documents that will assist other libraries in creating or revising their own strategic plans. The survey conducted for this CLIP Note collected detailed information on

2 - Introduction

strategic planning in college libraries and incorporates sample plans from 25 academic libraries, ranging from one-page strategic plans to documents offering more than 20 pages of detailed goals, objectives, action plans, timelines, and assessment measures.

SURVEY PROCEDURE

This study used the standard procedure for CLIP Notes projects. The initial proposal and draft of the questionnaire were submitted to the CLIP Notes Committee of ACRL's College Libraries Section, which reviewed and approved them. The survey tool was created on LimeSurvey, a service that allows respondents to complete an online questionnaire and facilitates compilation of results. In May 2010, emails with a link to the survey were sent to institutions agreeing to participate in the CLIP Notes series asking them to respond and to provide sample strategic plans. Two email reminders were sent to participating libraries, and a final round of phone calls were made to those who had not completed the survey. Collection of survey data was concluded in August 2010. Tabulation of the data results and selection of documents were completed in January 2011.

ANALYSIS OF SURVEY RESULTS

General information on survey respondents (Questions 2.1 – 3.5)

The survey link was emailed to 211 college and university libraries. A total of 134 useable surveys were collected, representing a response rate of 64%. While 26.9% of the respondents were public institutions, 73.1% were private. The majority (56%) of responding institutions was classified as Master's Colleges and Universities (small, medium, large), 41% were Baccalaureate Colleges, and 3% were Doctoral-granting institutions.

Institutional and library information was gathered in open-ended questions. For purposes of analysis, some survey data has been grouped in ranges for evaluation. Institutional enrollments ranged from 530 full time equivalent (FTE) students to 16,340 FTE students, with a median of 2,797 and a mean of 3,363. Institutions were grouped as follows:

Fewer than 2000 students – 34.3%
2000–3999 students – 35.1%
4000–5999 students – 19.4%
More than 6000 students – 11.2%

Faculty FTE ranged from 25 to 650, with a median of 170 and a mean of 196. Libraries had a mean of 7.8 FTE librarians and a median of 7, with a low of 1 librarian and a high of 19. FTE support staff in libraries ranged from 0 to 46, with a mean of 9.8 and a median of 8 staff employees.

There was a very diverse response to the number of volumes held by the libraries, from a low of 12,000 volumes to a high of 1,520,000 volumes, with a median of 244,943 and a mean of 322,295. Similarly, annual budget levels varied significantly, ranging from $250,000 to $6,906,142, with a mean of $1,815,495 and a median of $1,442,000. Annual budget (excluding salaries) ranged from $64,000 to $4,012,005, with a mean of $921,201 and a median of $695,359.

Strategic Plans (Questions 4.1 – 4.21)

Slightly more than half (54.5%) of responding libraries currently have strategic plans, while 45.5% reportedly have not developed strategic planning documents. Overall, 68% of responding public institutions had strategic plans, while only 50% of private institutions had plans. A potential explanation for this higher percentage of public institutions utilizing strategic planning may be found in survey respondents' demographic data, which shows that public institutions on average enroll twice as many students and have more faculty than private institutions with strategic plans. The survey data also indicate that public academic libraries have larger collections to manage. Another factor may be the higher dependence on state and federal funding, which in turn requires more planning and accountability.

The 61 libraries that do not currently have strategic plans were directed to the end of the survey questionnaire and probed on the reasons for not developing a plan and whether they intend to develop plans. The 73 libraries with strategic planning documents continued to complete the full survey, which solicited information on currency of plans; details in the reasons for developing plans and who was involved with writing, approving, and implementing the plans; the type of data covered by the plans; and how the plans align with institutional plans.

Clearly, libraries find it necessary to maintain the currency of their strategic plans: 95% percent of the libraries with plans reported that they developed or revised the planning documents within the last five years. In fact, 21.9% worked on the documents during the past year. Only three libraries currently had a strategic plan that was more than five years old. Another survey question asked how often the strategic planning document is reviewed and revised. The most common response (60.6%) was an annual review of the document, with an additional 14% reviewing every 1–3 years. This is supported by the literature, which suggests that the strategic planning process needs to be flexible, with frequent assessment and revision of action plans if necessary.

Survey respondents were queried regarding the top three motivating factors for developing their strategic plans. Respondents most frequently (91.8%) cited "planning for the library's future" as a motivating factor for developing a strategic plan. This response correlates closely with the fact that most of the plans are reviewed annually — the need to plan for the future corresponds to the dramatic changes libraries face in providing users with the services they need and affording institutions the value they expect. Half of the libraries noted that "improvement of services" was also a primary motivating factor. The other factors that received over one-third of respondents' support were "clarification of goals" (39.7%) and "responding to a campus directive" (34.2%). Issues that were infrequently identified as motivating factors for the decision to create a strategic plan were changes in mission, planning a new library, budgetary concerns, and changes in staffing.

Figure 1: What were the TOP 3 motivating factors for developing your library's strategic plan? (Choose 3)

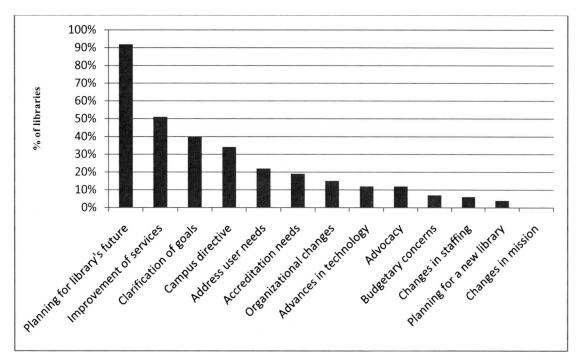

The next set of survey questions probed for more details on who participated in the development of library strategic plans. The responsibility for creating the strategic plan was most frequently a team effort. Only 19% of libraries indicated that an individual developed their plan, and a follow-up question revealed that the individual author was typically the Library Dean or Director. More than half (57.5%) of the libraries indicated that a committee was responsible for development of the strategic plan, and roughly half of those libraries formed a special committee for the task. Another 21.1% indicated that a regular faculty committee created the strategic plan. The size of the committees developing strategic plans was evenly divided: 40% indicated four to six people on the committee, while the same number had a committee of more than six individuals. Although library employees have primary responsibility for writing strategic plans, a number of libraries also involved college teaching faculty, students, library advisory boards, and college administrators in the writing process. It is logical to conclude that the majority of libraries sought broad-based support for the goals identified since they used committees and many involved library employees at all levels. The planning process facilitates communication and participation by involving those who are expected to execute the strategic plan.

Figure 2: Who was involved in writing your library's strategic plan? (Choose all that apply)

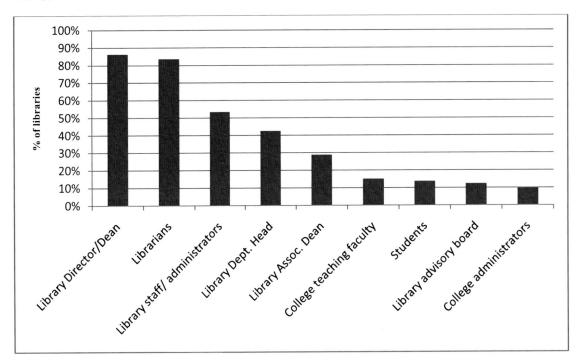

The type of academic faculty involvement in creating libraries' strategic plans varied among respondents. While only six libraries had academic faculty on the writing team, faculty offered assistance in developing strategic plans in several roles: provided input to plans (39.7%), reviewed drafts of plans (37%), and approved plans (13.7%). Several libraries also mentioned faculty serving on a library committee and participating in focus groups. Since faculty play a critical role in encouraging students to utilize library services, their input and review of plans solidifies support for the library and provides an important outside perspective of both faculty and student needs.

The Library Director/Dean adopted or approved the strategic plan in three quarters of responding libraries. Almost half of the libraries (47.9%) noted that librarians approved the plan, while one third of the libraries mentioned that library staff was involved in the approval process. Again, approval of the strategic plan by library employees reinforces buy-in from those who will need to carry out the objectives or action plans. The desire to develop strategic plans for the library that reflect broader institutional goals was evident, as slightly more than half (56.3%) received approval for the plans from the Chief Academic Officer/Provost, an additional 15.5% received approval from the College President, and 4.2% were approved by the college's Board of Directors.

The amount of time needed to develop strategic plans ranged from less than one month to more than one year, with one third of libraries completing the process in fewer than three months, and an additional 31% requiring 4–6 months to develop a strategic plan. The number of people involved in the writing process did not affect the amount of time spent on developing the strategic plan, which was similar for individuals and committees.

6 - Introduction

Currency of strategic plans is essential, and planning beyond a five-year period is rarely done. Slightly more than three quarters (77.1%) of the libraries developed strategic plans that cover a 3–5 year timeframe. An additional 13% of libraries created plans that address anticipated needs over the next two years. A subsequent question also probed the frequency of reviews and revisions of the strategic plan. As the literature suggests, currency is important: 60% of libraries review plans annually, with an additional 12.7% indicating review as needed. The remaining 25% of libraries indicated reviews between one and five years. Flexibility and adjustments to reflect environmental changes are critical. As some objectives are completed, new goals may be added.

Strategic planning documents cover a multitude of areas that are critical in the operation of an academic library. Based on the responses, more than one half of the libraries indicated that they addressed 16 of the 18 areas enumerated in the survey question. All libraries included goals and objectives in their documents, and 94.4% also included mission statements. Scholarly communication and user expectations were the only two areas that fewer than half of the libraries discussed in their plans. Some of the items mentioned under the "other" category included assessment, information literacy, ACRL standards, and SWOT analysis. The following chart details topics covered.

Figure 3:What areas are addressed in your library's strategic plan?(Choose all that apply)

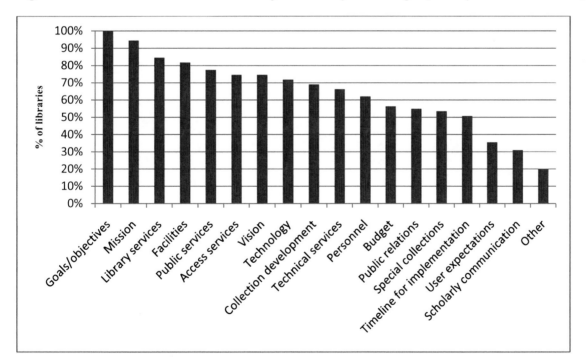

In terms of document length, 30% of the responding libraries developed a plan fewer than five pages in length. Another 42.9% have plans that are 5 to 10 pages. Nine libraries revealed their plans were 21 to 50 pages, and only two libraries had plans longer than 50 pages. Looking at the sample documents provided by respondents, it is evident that most libraries creating documents fewer than 20 pages in length format their reports in a succinct, bulleted fashion —

listing goals, objectives and action items. Longer documents are more likely to include an analysis of the library's current status, supported by library statistics and professional data.

Implementation of the strategic plans falls primarily on the shoulders of the Library Director/Dean in 97% of libraries. However, just under half also responded that librarians or department heads are accountable for implementation of strategic plans. Furthermore, 80% of the libraries have a procedure in place for assessment of success in achieving goals identified in the plans.

Ninety percent of the libraries identified library employees as the audience for the strategic planning document. Moreover, the strategic plan plays an important role in raising awareness on campus regarding the library's future directions; almost three quarters of the respondents also felt that the campus community was an intended audience for the report. The plans are also provided to accreditation associations by 42% of the libraries.

Libraries often take a multi-pronged approach to dissemination of their strategic plan, using both print and electronic distribution. The most common distribution was in electronic format to library employees. Forty-five percent of libraries post their strategic plan on their website, and the same number said they provide the plan on an "as-needed" basis. A smaller number distribute plans outside the library, either in print or electronic format.

Figure 4: How is the strategic plan made available? (Choose all that apply)

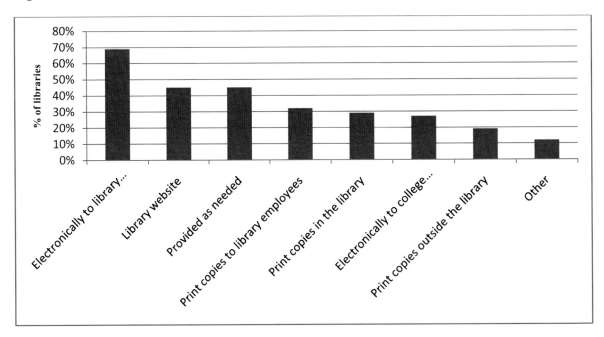

All survey respondents were asked whether an accreditation association had asked for or recommended the development of a strategic plan. Only 14% of libraries replied that they were asked about a strategic plan. Fifty-four percent had not been asked for a plan, and 28% did not know whether a strategic plan had been requested for the library. However, as mentioned earlier, 42% of libraries did elect to provide their strategic plan as part of their institutional input to accreditation associations.

The perceived value of strategic plans was probed in a survey question that asked the respondents to rate the importance of the document in providing direction for their library. On a scale of 1 to 5, with one being very important, slightly more than half (52%) rated importance at the highest level. An additional 28% of libraries rated importance at "2." At the other end of the spectrum, only 1 library felt the plan was not important and 11% rated it at a level "4" in importance.

The 61 survey respondents who did not have a strategic plan in place were queried regarding reasons for not developing a plan. Seventy percent of libraries without plans indicated they were following their college's strategic plan. Five libraries felt it would not be useful, and five libraries replied that it was too time-consuming to create a plan. Thirty percent of the respondents provided their own reasons for not having a strategic plan, such as: annual report is sufficient for planning, perform short-term planning, and staff resistance to long-term planning. Several individual comments were tied to institutional plans under development.

Respondents without strategic plans were queried regarding potential development of strategic plans for their libraries. Thirty-one percent of the libraries currently have plans under development or will develop plans within the next year. An analysis of the 30 libraries that do not plan to develop strategic plans revealed that more than three-quarters of those follow college plans.

Conclusions

A review of the survey data indicates that libraries who currently have a strategic plan are more likely to have the following profile:
- public colleges,
- enroll more than 2000 students,
- have more than 200 faculty members,
- employ more than 7 librarians and more than 5 support staff,
- hold more than 300,000 volumes, and
- expend an annual library budget (including salaries) of more than $2,000,000.

Based on survey responses, the primary value of strategic plans is to provide direction for library employees and, secondarily, to create awareness of the library on campus. The need to offer new services, especially electronic resources, even when faced with decreased funding, makes the strategic plan an effective management tool for library advocacy. The strategic planning process takes the library's vision and translates it into goals and objectives, as well as creates a roadmap to attain end results and achieve success. Plans are typically developed to provide direction for a five-year period, although the plans are reviewed regularly. The frequency of the updates is likely to coincide with annual assessments measuring the success in achieving the goals and objectives defined in the strategic plans.

As is illustrated in the strategic planning documents provided by respondents for inclusion in this CLIP Note, the format for strategic planning documents produced by libraries varies greatly both in document type and level of detail provided for goals and objectives. Document types include word documents, PDFs, spreadsheets, brochures, and online versions. In terms of document organization, at the top level all of the documents provide "strategies," "goals," or areas of "focus" that serve as initiatives to be achieved by the libraries. The next level of definition is typically "objectives" or "action plans" of how these goals will be addressed in the individual libraries. Some libraries also provide timeframes for implementation, assignment of specific tasks to departments or individuals, and potential evaluation measures. Several of the longer documents also provide information on the library's current status in strategic areas and benefits of achieving the plan's goals.

Thirty-nine respondents offered documents for inclusion in this publication. A representative selection of the strategic planning documents (or excerpts) have been included in this CLIP Note to provide guidance to libraries either developing new strategic plans or revising their current documents.

SELECTED BIBLIOGRAPHY

Birdsall, Douglas G., "Strategic Planning in Academic Libraries: A Political Perspective." ACRL, Publications in Librarianship, Academic Libraries. http://www.ala.org/ala/mgrps/divs/acrl/publications/booksmonographs/pil/pil49/birdsall.cfm

Brown, Walter A. and Blake Gonzalez, Barbara A., "Academic Libraries: Should Strategic Planning be Renewed?" *Technical Services Quarterly* 24, no.3 (2007): 1–14.

Butler, Meredith, and Davis, Hiram, "Strategic Planning as a Catalyst for Change in the 1990's." *College and Research Libraries* 53, no.5 (1992): 393–403.

Clement, Richard W. *SPEC Kit #210, Strategic Planning in ARL Libraries.* Association for Research Libraries: Washington, D.C. 1995.

Decker, Reinhold and Hoppner, Michael, "Strategic Planning and Customer Intelligence in Academic Libraries." *Library Hi Tech* 24, no. 4 (2006): 504–14.

Dougherty, Richard M., "Planning for a New Library Future." *Library Journal* 127, no.9 (2002): 38–41.

Franklin, Brinley, "Aligning Library Strategy and Structure with the Campus Academic Plan: A Case Study." *Journal of Library Administration* 49, no. 5 (July 2009): 495–505.

Little, Jennifer J. and Huten, Jan H., "Strategic Planning: First Steps in Sharing Information Literacy Goals with Faculty Across Disciplines." *College & Undergraduate Libraries* 13 no.3 (2006): 113–23.

Matthews, Joseph R., *Strategic Planning and Management for Library Managers.* Libraries Unlimited: Westport, CT. 2005.

Miller, Julie L., "Reinventing the Library at Eastern Washington University: An Intensive Strategic Planning Experience with Faculty." *Technical Services Quarterly* 26, no.2 (2009): 96–106.

Morein, P. Grady, "What is a CLIP Note?" *College and Research Libraries News* 46 (1985): 226–29.

Nelson, Sandra, *Implementing for Results: From Ideas to Action.* ALA: Chicago. 2008.

Nelson, Sandra, *Strategic Planning for Results.* ALA: Chicago. 2008.

Oberembt, Kenneth, *Annual Reports for College Libraries, CLIP Note #10.* ALA: Chicago. 1988.

Pacios, Ana R., "Strategic Plans and Long-Range Plans: Is There a Difference? " *Library Management* 25, no.6/7 (2004): 259–69.

Riggs, Donald E., *Strategic Planning for Library Managers*. Oryx Press: Phoenix. 1984.

Ryan, Susan M., "Library Web Site Administration: A Strategic Planning Model for the Smaller Academic Library." *The Journal of Academic Librarianship* 29, no. 4 (July 2003): 207–18.

Sauer, James, "The Annual Report: The Academic Librarian's Tool for Management, Strategic Planning, and Advocacy." *College & Undergraduate Libraries* 13, no.2 (2006): 21–34.

Schulz, Lisa, "Strategic Planning in a University Library." *Marketing Library Services* 12, no.5 (July/August 1998). http://www.infotoday.com/mls/jul98/story.htm

SURVEY RESULTS

Respondent Information

1.1 **Institution name**	(134 responses)
1.2 **Institution's address**	(134 responses)
1.3 **Name of respondent**	(134 responses)
1.4 **Respondent's title**	(134 responses)
1.5 **Respondent's work telephone number**	(134 responses)
1.6 **Respondent's email address**	(134 responses)
1.7 **Respondent's fax number**	(134 responses)

Institutional Data

2.1 Carnegie classification

(Please choose only one of the following)   (134 responses)

- 33 (24.6%) Master's/M: Master's Colleges and Universities (medium programs)
- 37 (27.6%) Master's/S: Master's Colleges and Universities (smaller programs)
- 39 (29.1%) Bac/A&S: Baccalaureate Colleges – Arts & Sciences
- 15 (11.2%) Bac/Diverse: Baccalaureate Colleges – Diverse Fields
- 2 (01.5%) Bac/Diverse: Baccalaureate/Associate's Colleges
- 8 (06.0%) Other:
  - Masters (large program) – 4
  - Doctoral – 4

2.2 Type of institution

(Please choose only one of the following)   (134 responses)

- 36 (26.9%) Public
- 98 (73.1%) Private

2.3 Number of full-time equivalent (FTE) students   (134 responses)

- 46 (34.3%) Fewer than 2000 students
- 47 (35.1%) 2000–3999
- 26 (19.4%) 4000–5999
- 15 (11.2%) 6000+ students

Median= 2797   Mean = 3363   Range: 530 to 16,340

2.4 Number of full-time equivalent (FTE) faculty   (129 responses)

- 27 (20.9%) Fewer than 100 FTE faculty
- 46 (35.7%) 100–199
- 49 (38.0%) 200–399
- 7 (05.4%) 400+ faculty

Median= 170   Mean = 196   Range: 25 to 650

Library Information

3.1 Number of full-time equivalent (FTE) librarians   (134 responses)
     28 (20.9%) Fewer than 5 FTE librarians
     35 (27.1%) 5–6.9
     18 (13.4%) 7–8.9
     25 (18.7%) 9–10.9
     28 (20.9%) 11 + FTE Librarians

     Median= 7   Mean = 7.8   Range: 1 to 19

3.2 Number of full-time equivalent (FTE) support staff   (134 responses)
     34 (25.4%) Fewer than 5 FTE Support staff
     34 (25.4%) 5–8.9
     31 (23.1%) 9–12.9
     25 (18.7%) 13–19.9
     10 (07.5%) 20 + FTE Support staff

     Median= 8   Mean = 9.8   Range: 0 to 46

3.3 Number of volumes   (131 responses)
     Median= 244,943   Mean = 322,395   Range: 12,000 to 1,520,012

3.4 Library's annual budget (including salaries)   (117 responses)
     Median= $1,422,000 Mean = $1,815,495   Range: $250,000 to $6,906,142

3.5 Library's annual budget (excluding salaries)   (121 responses)
     Median= $695,359   Mean = $921,201   Range: $64,000 to $4,012,005

Strategic Planning

4.1 Do you currently have a strategic plan for your Library?   (134 responses)
     73 (54.5%) Yes
     61 (45.5%) No

4.2 How long ago was your strategic plan created/revised?
     (Choose only one)   (73 responses)
     16 (21.9%) Less than one year
     24 (32.9%) 1–2 years
     29 (39.7%) 3–5 years
      2 (02.7%) 6–10 years
      1 (01.4%) More than 10 years
      1 (01.4%) Don't know

4.3 What were the TOP 3 motivating factors for developing your library's strategic plan?
     (Choose 3)   (73 responses)
     67 (91.8%) Planning for the library's future
     37 (50.7%) Improvement of services
     29 (39.7%) Clarification of goals
     25 (34.2%) Campus directive
     16 (21.6%) Address user needs
     14 (19.2%) Accreditation needs

11 (15.1%) Organizational changes
9 (12.3%) Advances in technology
9 (12.3%) Advocacy — create awareness on campus
5 (06.8%) Budgetary concerns
4 (05.5%) Changes in staffing
3 (04.1%) Planning new library
0 (00.0%) Changes in mission
4 (05.5%) Other:
    1 Campus-wide strategic planning
    1 Planning renovations
    1 Desire for innovation
    1 Integrating library with other campus programs

4.4 Does your library's strategic plan align with the college's strategic plan?

(73 responses)

68 (93.2%) Yes
5 (06.8%) No

4.5 Who was responsible for creating your strategic plan?

(Choose all that apply)   (73 responses)
14 (19.2%) Individual
42 (57.5%) Committee
24 (34.2%) Other:
    13 All librarians and staff/everyone
     4 Librarians
     4 Library management team
     1 Director's advisory team
     1 Departments
     1 All staff who wished to participate

4.5a Who was the author of your library's strategic planning document?

(If individual author)   (14 responses)
14 (100%) Library Director/Dean
 0 (0.0%) Library Assistant Director
 0 (0.0%) Library Assistant/Associate Dean
 0 (0.0%) Library Department Head
 0 (0.0%) Librarian

4.5b Who served on the strategic planning committee?

(If committee, choose all that apply)   (42 responses)
22 (52.4%) Specially formed strategic planning committee
11 (21.2%) Regular library faculty committee
 3 (07.1%) 1–3 people
17 (40.5%) 4–6 people
17 (40.5%) More than 6 people
 2 (04.8%) Other:
    1 Librarians and staff
    1 Regular committee and student member

4.6 Who was involved in writing your library's strategic plan?

(Choose all that apply) (73 responses)

63 (86.3%) Library Director/Dean
61 (83.6%) Librarians
39 (53.4%) Library staff/administrators
31 (42.5%) Library Department Head
21 (28.8%) Library Associate/Assistant Dean or Assistant Director
11 (15.1%) College teaching faculty
10 (13.7%) Students
9 (12.3%) Library advisory board
7 (09.6%) College administrators (outside of library)
0 (00.0%) Other

4.7 What was the level of academic faculty involvement in developing the strategic plan?

(Please choose all that apply) (71 responses)

29 (39.7%) Provided input to plan
27 (37.0%) Reviewed draft of plan
25 (34.0%) None
10 (13.7%) Approved plan
6 (08.2%) Part of the writing team
4 (05.5%) Other:
  1 Library committee made up of academic faculty, students/librarians
  1 Through faculty library committee
  1 Reviewed final plan
  1 Involved in focus group

4.8 Approximately how long did it take to develop the strategic plan from initial draft to adoption?

(Please choose only one) (71 responses)

4 (05.6%) Less than one month
20 (28.2%) 1–3 months
22 (31.0%) 4–6 months
17 (23.9%) 7–12 months
6 (08.5%) More than one year
0 (00.0%) Don't know
2 (02.8%) Other:
  1 Various over the years
  1 Planning has many parts, cannot answer

4.9 Who adopted or approved the strategic plan?

(Choose all that apply) (71 responses)

53 (74.6%) Library Director/Dean
40 (56.3%) Chief academic officer/Provost
34 (47.9%) Librarians
23 (32.4%) Library staff
13 (18.3%) Library administrators
11 (15.5%) College president
5 (07.0%) College faculty
3 (04.2%) Board of trustees
1 (01.4%) Don't know
7 (09.9%) Other:

       3   Library committee
       2   Institutional effectiveness committee
       1   Strategic planning committee
       1   University assessment office
       1   Campus strategic planning committee
       1   In process

4.10 What is the timeframe covered by the strategic plan?
(Please choose only one)   (70 responses)
       1   (01.4%)   Less than one year
       8   (11.4%)   1–2 years
      54   (77.1%)   3–5 years
       5   (07.1%)   6–10 years
       0   (00.0%)   More than 10 years
       2   (02.9%)   Other:
                     1   No timeframe
                     1   Open-ended

4.11 What areas are addressed in your library's strategic plan?
(Choose all that apply)   (71 responses)
      71   (100%)   Goals and objectives
      67   (94.4%)   Mission
      60   (84.5%)   Library services
      58   (81.7%)   Facilities
      55   (77.5%)   Public services (reference, instruction)
      53   (74.6%)   Vision
      53   (74.6%)   Access services (circulation, ILL)
      51   (71.8%)   Technology
      49   (69.0%)   Collection development
      47   (66.2%)   Technical services
      44   (62.0%)   Personnel
      40   (56.3%)   Budget
      39   (54.9%)   Public relations
      38   (53.5%)   Special collections
      37   (52.1%)   Collaboration/resource sharing
      36   (50.7%)   Timeline for implementation
      26   (36.6%)   User expectations
      22   (31.0%)   Scholarly communication
      14   (19.7%)   Other:
                     3   Assessment
                     2   Information literacy
                     1   SWOT Analysis
                     1   ACRL standards
                     1   Program direction
                     1   Marketing
                     1   Staff development
                     1   Public engagement
                     1   Measurement
                     1   Digicenter
                     1   Community service

4.12 Who is responsible for the implementation of the strategic plan?
(Choose all that apply)   (71 responses)
69 (97.2%) Library Director/Dean
10 (14.1%) Library Assistant Director
 8 (11.3%) Library Assistant/Associate Dean
33 (46.5%) Library Department Head
35 (49.3%) Librarian
 7 (01.4%) Strategic planning committee
16 (22.5%) Other:
       9   All library employees
       3   Library faculty
       1   Management team
       1   Library cabinet
       1   Library administrative and support staff
       1   Chairs of library committees created by plan
       1   Advisory group to the Library Director

4.13 Is there a plan in place for assessment of success in achieving goals? (71 responses)
57 (80.3%) Yes
14 (19.7%) No

4.14 How often is the strategic planning document reviewed/revised?
(Please choose all that apply)   (71 responses)
43 (60.6%) Annually
10 (14.1%) 1–3 years
 8 (11.3%) 4–5 years
 1 (01.4%) 6–10 years
 1 (01.4%) During accreditation
 2 (12.7%) As needed
 2 (02.8%) Other:
       1   Overdue for revision
       1   Throughout the year

4.15 What is the length of the strategic planning document?
(Please choose only one)   (70 responses)
21 (30.0%) Fewer than 5 pages
30 (42.9%) 5–10 pages
 6 (08.6%) 11–20 pages
 9 (12.9%) 21–50 pages
 2 (02.9%) More than 50 pages
 0 (00.0%) Don't know
 2 (02.9%) Other
       1   Still in writing stage
       1   Online through planning software

4.16 Who is the intended audience for your library's strategic plan?

(Please choose all that apply)   (71 responses)

64 (90.1%) Library employees
52 (73.2%) College campus
30 (42.3%) Accreditation association
 9 (12.7%) Other
      3 Senior/college administrators
      1 VPAA
      1 Trustees
      1 State library board
      1 President and officers of the university
      1 Other libraries, also IT department
      1 Continuous improvement of campus

4.17 How important is the strategic planning document in providing direction for your library?

(Please choose only one)   (71 responses)

1= Very important				5= not important
1	**2**	**3**	**4**	**5**
37	20	5	8	1
52.1%	28.2%	7.0%	11.3%	1.4%

4.18 How is the strategic plan made available?

(Please choose all that apply)   (71 responses)

21 (29.6%) Print copies in the library
23 (32.4%) Print copies distributed to library employees
14 (19.4%) Print copies distributed outside the library
32 (45.1%) Posted to the library's website
49 (69.0%) Electronically to library employees
19 (26.7%) Electronically to college employees/students
32 (45.1%) Provided as needed
 9 (12.7%) Other:
- Will be distributed in different format through website and available to campus through the planning software package
- The college's common drive
- Print copy to Dean for Academic Affairs
- Part of annual report
- Mission on the Library web site
- Integrated into online Campus Balanced Scorecard
- Incorporated into institutional plan
- Electronically to VP for Academic Administration and to Library Committee
- Electronically to academic councils

4.19 Has an accreditation association ever asked for or recommended the development of a strategic plan for your library?

(Please choose only one)   (129 responses)

18 (14.0%) Yes
70 (54.3%) No
36 (27.9%) Don't know
 5 (03.9%) Other:
- Accreditation association is requiring an overall planning and assessment project of which the library is part
- They asked to see our strategic plan
- These are two separate questions. MSA has seen our plan which has been in existence for close to 20 years.
- Strategic Plan submitted for HLC reaccreditation but not requested
- Part of college's strategic plan

4.20 For libraries without strategic plans, which were reasons for not developing a plan?

(Please choose all that apply)   (61 responses)

43 (70.5%) Follow college's strategic plan
 5 (08.2%) Not being perceived as being useful
 5 (08.2%) Too time consuming to create
19 (31.1%) Other
- Currently under development
- While we may not have felt the need for one up to this time, I think that we will be likely to undertake one in the next few years.
- We will be doing one in the near future
- We drafted a strategic plan and sent it forward to the Provost; were told to wait until after the college-wide strategic plan had been implemented.
- We do short range planning and careful assessment, but have relied on larger college plan in past; we will participate actively in a new strategic plan being formulated campus wide during the next 6 months
- The library employs an ongoing three-year planning process. Since assessment is tied to this process, there's ample opportunity to develop strategic initiatives.
- The Library and Information Services division develops an annual plan that outlines specific objectives that are directly tied to the College's strategic plan.
- Staff resistance to long term planning
- Outdated plan
- Not sure
- Need the university to develop and adopt a clear strategic plan first. Our strategic plan should be supportive of the university's.
- Library is in the process of merging with another library and combining collections

- Involved in a planning process that may or may not use this specific model
- In process of developing with college's plan
- I am new and cannot explain why it hasn't been done in the past.
- Has not been implemented
- Change in leadership

4.21 When will your library develop a strategic plan?

(Please choose only one)   (61 responses)

30 (49.2%)	No plans to develop a strategic plan
8 (13.1%)	Plan is currently under development
11 (18.0%)	Within one year
9 (14.8%)	2–5 years
2 (03.3%)	Other

    1   Since the current University Librarian is retiring, a new director may feel it is time for strategic planning

    1   We may develop a strategic plan but haven't decided for sure

DOCUMENTS

Strategic Plan

Vision Statement

In support of the mission and strategic plan of Augustana College, the Thomas Tredway Library develops and promotes access to information. In collaboration with the teaching faculty, the library staff selects and facilitates access to all forms and formats of information, and instructs in the uses, interpretation and evaluation of information so that Augustana students will be prepared for citizenship and leadership in our changing world. The library endeavors to create and nurture a place on the college campus that supports intellectual curiosity and encourages the on-going exchange of ideas. The library seeks to provide an environment that promotes respect, diversity, and intellectual growth and excellence.

Goals

Materials—Support and enrich each student's learning with the most educationally valuable resources in the most appropriate formats.

Organization—Make the library simple to use; describe and organize knowledge and information so that users can obtain resources in the most efficient manner.

Service—Deliver coordinated, consistent, and high quality service that is responsive to the Augustana community and to other library users.

Teaching—Collaborate with the faculty to teach each Augustana student to locate, evaluate, and use information effectively.

Place—Develop the library not only as a repository of resources or a gateway to information, but as a place where faculty, staff, and students communicate and collaborate intellectually, culturally, and socially; enhance the library to best support Augustana's goals of academic excellence and student growth.

Community— Contribute to the development of the Augustana College community by participating in its curricular and co-curricular activities, and in its connections to the greater community.

Communication—Inform the college community what we do and why; engage the members of that community in using library services, thereby promoting the integration of intellectual inquiry, academic excellence, and respect for diversity into the fabric of Augustana College.

Professional Development—Participate in professional communities and activities in order to strengthen the services of the library and their support of academic excellence.

BATES COLLEGE: INFORMATION AND LIBRARY SERVICES > PROJECTS & INITIATIVES

Strategic Plan 2007-2010s

Update to 1999 ILS Strategic Plan

ILS will build a high quality and service-oriented library and computing organization providing outstanding support for information and technology needs of the campus. It will help users manage continuous change in modes of information use, information access, and communications media and technology. This will be done by working on the following strategic objectives:

1. Develop ubiquitous and reliable computing and information access on the campus. Continue to support progressively increasing capacity on wired network and provide wireless in an expanding number of places. Build the campus technology infrastructure to be redundant and fault tolerant. This technology infrastructure development will be integrated with the implementation of the Campus Master Plan. Through established replacement plans, assure timely replacement of computers, media equipment, servers, network devices and other related technologies.
2. Provide outstanding support of the information needs of the Bates curriculum. Manage the transformation of library collections to a mixed print and electronic environment where electronic sources play an increasingly important role. Expect the transition to electronic formats for library and College information to accelerate. Instructional programs to help users sift through large amounts of information will be increasingly important, both for licensed collections and free Internet materials. Some new and exciting information tools will require new software and/or hardware – connect these decisions as effectively as possible.
3. Continue to strengthen technology-related services to faculty members and provide leadership for educational initiatives when appropriate. Develop flexible approaches that meet educational objectives, and facilitate learning among faculty members of new technologies and new ideas.
4. Strengthen integrated computing environment to support the business and communication functions of the College based on a centralized secure database. Continue to add secure Web-enabled applications to extend the functionality directly to users. Pay particular attention to efficiency, identifying opportunities to use automation to reduce human data entry, duplication of effort and unnecessary paperwork. A document image management and a data warehouse strategy for the College will be needed.
5. Continue to strengthen facilities and resources for use of archives and special collections. Establish a records management function for paper, electronic, and other media.
6. Develop high quality, secure and cost-effective solutions to support mobile technologies. Ubiquity of the network, especially with wireless access, will support a wide array of mobile devices. Which ones do we support, and for what purposes? Students should be encouraged, rewarded and supported in using their own computing devices, relying on College-owned equipment only when necessary.
7. Continue to expand use of the Web as a delivery mechanism for more communications, data access, teaching and learning.

8. Continue to explore ways to simplify the computing environment through standardization of software packages and reduction of duplicative resources. Work closely with faculty members in this area to assure learning objectives are met.
9. Pay increasing attention to data security, protection of privacy, ethical use of data, and secure human practices in data use. This includes authentication systems for easy and secure access to official and licensed information. This is as much an educational issue as it is a technology issue.
10. Build collaborative relationships with partners outside Bates. The CBB consortium a cornerstone of library services of the College. Extend partnerships with library and information technology organizations in other colleges, particularly for functions where distance is not an obstacle to effective service delivery. Increase participation in open-source software development and deployment.
11. Establish effective management and stewardship of information and technology resources. Develop transparent budgeting and priority-setting processes with faculty, staff and student involvement. The need for assessment and accountability will be increasingly important for both planning and operations. Bates will actively participate in development of effective tools for assessment of technology and library services, including output and outcomes measures. Staff will continue to be both effective in what they do and accountable for their work.
12. Work within framework established for implementation of the Campus Facilities Master Plan to improve work space for ILS, especially by reducing the number of staff locations.
13. Strengthen efforts to seek outside support through grants, individual philanthropy and other funding opportunities.

February 19, 2007

Karl E. Mundt Library & Information Commons

DSU Institutional Effectiveness Committee
Strategic Plan Presentation
March 4, 2008

Our Library Mission

- The **mission** of the Karl E. Mundt Library & Learning Commons is to supply the library and information needs of the students, staff, and faculty of Dakota State University and to support the University's stated mission and goals.

- **Information Literacy: DSU students should be able to find, evaluate and use information for problem solving and decision making in all aspects of their lives -- at home, in the workplace, and as informed citizens in a democratic society.**

The **overarching goal** of the Mundt is to provide online and physical services and environments to support student academic, social, and personal success.
We seek to focus the activities of the Mundt so that the University's mission and the campus strategic plan are supported and advanced.

What follows are the special projects we plan for the upcoming year in support of the strategic plan – Dakota State University: Focused.

Dakota State University's 2007-2012 strategic plan reflects the following set of values and shared commitments to:
    The use of data-informed decision making to improve and enrich the university's programs.

- **Library Goal 1**: By 2012 we will be able to easily answer the following accreditation question "How does the Mundt contribute to campus life, student learning, and teaching effectiveness?" and prove it with data.

- **Library Objective 1**: By Spring 2009, identify and establish appropriate benchmarks measures for monitoring Library impact on campus life, student learning and teaching effectiveness and create a Library Dashboard.

    Potential Evaluation Measures: Part of developing this objective will be determining what our meaningful data is. Assessment data – General Education Goal #7, ACRL Statistics (comparison with peers) Suggestion-box (real & virtual) suggestions, Data from institutional inventories & surveys, Student satisfaction with library services (Noel Levitz Student Satisfaction Inventory), Number of programs, Communications to students, Usability study of speed of task performance & subjective user satisfaction, Time to process requests, increased usage statistics, expanded information services, and improved facilities; increased content on Library homepage, the extended and on campus library services ratings, assessment data. We provide evidence of a facility focused on being student-centered and fostering collaborative learning.

Dakota State University's 2007-2012 strategic plan reflects the following set of values and shared commitments to:
An unwavering support for student success and learning by promoting active engagement and creative problem-solving.

- **Library Goal 2: By 2012, t**he Library will routinely assess and improve its online information literacy instruction program to insure it meets the needs of on and off campus students.

- **Library Objective 2:** By May 2009, the present online information literacy tutorial will be evaluated and changes will be implemented.

  Potential Evaluation Measures: Assessment Data – General Ed. Goal #7; Student evaluation surveys, focus groups.

Strategic Focus #1: Focus On Expanding Information Technology Leadership
Refine and expand its on -campus and state-wide leadership in
creating exceptionally effective mobile computing environments.

- **Library Goal 3**: Integrate appropriate social technologies into various aspects of the library's activities.

- **Library Objective 3:** By Spring 2009, the Library will implement federated searching across multiple databases.

  Potential Evaluation Measures: Either implemented or not, Usage data

Strategic Focus #1: Focus On Expanding Information Technology Leadership
Refine and expand its on -campus and state-wide leadership in
creating exceptionally effective mobile computing environments.

- **Library Goal 4**: By 2012, the Library will have established the necessary policies, processes and procedures necessary to participate in the new SD Digital Library. (create digital collections from some of the unique and rare holdings of the University & Foundation Archives)

- **Library Objective 4:** By Fall 2008, the Library will have identified and prioritized collections for inclusion in the South Dakota Digital Library (and actively participate in the developmental conversations of the SDDL)

  Potential Evaluation Measures: annual report on potential digitization projects, benchmark set, or other data points established.

Strategic Focus #7: Focus On Developing New Financial Resources
   Obtain funding to support facilities and campus infrastructure improvements.

- **Library Goal 5**: The Library will identify potential funding sources to support the costs for creating digital collections from some of the unique and rare holdings of the University & Foundation Archives

- **Library Objective** 5: By Spring 2009, the Library will have submitted one digitization grant application

   Potential Evaluation Measures: Application, list of possible funding sources

Strategic Focus #7: Focus On Developing New Financial Resources
   Obtain funding to support facilities and campus infrastructure improvements.

- **Library Goal 6**: The Library will identify potential funding sources to support the costs for creating new library programming and displays

- **Library Objective** 6: By May 2009, the Library will have submitted at least one programming/display grant application

   Potential Evaluation Measures: Application, list of possible funding sources

Strategic Focus #7: Focus On Developing New Financial Resources
   Increase campus efficiencies by "going green".

- EcoPhone Recycling

- **Library Goal 7**: The Library will identify and implement a recycling project.

- **Library Objective** 7: By May 2008, a pilot recycling project will be implemented

   Potential Evaluation Measures: Report, revenue generated

DSU Strategic Focus #3: Focus On Retention and Graduation by Providing an Exceptional Student Experience
   Improve campus life with an expanded menu of meaningful and more diverse academic, cultural, and student life events.

- **Library Goal 8**: The Library will implement and evaluate its programs and displays.

- **Library Objective** 8: By January 2009, the Library will identify campus partners to develop and implement a "One Book, One Campus" project.

   Potential Evaluation Measures: Book identified, Guidelines developed, Number of participants, Partners identified,

Dakota State University

Strategic Focus #5: Focus On Extending Educational Outreach
    Review online processes and services to address the unique needs of undergraduate and graduate distance students.

- **Library Goal 9**: The Library will review its processes, services, and communications to ensure that they meet the needs of students on campus and off, undergraduate and graduate.

- **Library Objective** 9a: By December 2008, all policies and procedures related to resource sharing (ILL) will be reviewed and updated.

- **Library Objective** 9b: By May 2009, all policies and procedures related to circulation will be reviewed and updated.

Potential Evaluation Measures: report, benchmarks established

LIBRARY STRATEGIC FIVE-YEAR PLAN – 2009-2014
6/4/09

GOAL ONE: To provide collections, services, and programs to assist faculty, students, and staff in achieving the educational objectives of the university.

Objective 1.1: Organize the resources of the library efficiently and effectively and provide user-friendly access to materials in all formats.
  a. Celebrate 300,000th volume, and five years later 350,000th!
  b. Use Millennium modules to their capacity – implement automatic ordering, test use of commercial cataloging records, and develop system for faculty notification.
  c. Develop a cost management plan to respond pro-actively to budget situations.
  d. Develop and implement Innovative equipment maintenance and replacement plan.
  e. Analyze approval plan results and implement change as indicated.
  f. Provide timely access to audiovisual materials for classroom use. Expand streaming video and online audio resources. Consider a booking system.
  g. Investigate patron tagging in the online catalog and other social networking applications.
  h. Review microforms collection for retention. Consider changes in equipment and space allocation.
  i. Consider implementing a book/AV delivery system for faculty and staff.

Objective 1.2: Create library facilities that respond to student needs, are technologically current and sustainable, house materials adequately, and support efforts to build a campus community.
  a. Complete book storage plan and submit to Dr. Lambert.
  b. Complete relocation of books to Elon West and improve stacks management systems for shifting and shelving.
  c. Develop building program for library addition/renovation. Include storage, programmatic, study, office spaces and possible coffee shop.
  d. Review information desk staffing patterns and modify as indicated.
  e. Working with Campus Safety and Police and with Student Life, improve security of valuables, students, and staff in Belk Library.
  f. Work with Sustainability Coordinator to improve recycling and energy reduction initiatives.

Objective 1.3: Hire, develop and retain a highly qualified library staff.
  a. Write new five-year staffing plan for submission to administration (web designer, digitization librarian, weekend staffing?).
  b. Investigate staffing patterns, job descriptions, and administrative organization to ensure effectiveness in the 21st century. Implement recommendations.
  c. Continue to improve student worker development, organization, and training.
  d. Create staff development plans for all library staff.
      a. Implement new evaluation form for librarians. Consider role of publication, research, presentations, and service.
  e. Implement formal cross-training program, particularly among student workers and support staff.
  f. Continue "Library 2.0 Committee" for the ongoing investigation of new technologies. Consult with librarians at peer and aspirant institutions.
  g. Plan for leadership change within 2-4 years.

h. Successfully recruit candidates to participate in diversity grant received from the Institute of Museum and Library Services and coordinated by UNC-Greensboro. Provide internship and possibly short-term post-degree employment.

Objective 1.4: Expand library use by students as measured by circulation, interlibrary loan, reference, in-house and online usage, and building usage statistics.
a. Continually review library hours and staffing patterns for both effectiveness and efficiency. Review hours for Winter Term, summer and breaks. Analyze statistics and make recommendations to Dr. Wise.
b. Develop clear benchmarks for measuring "success."
c. Increase usage of resources by 10% over the next five years.
d. In consultation with on-campus graduate programs, improve both on-campus and distance support of graduate students as measured by usage, student surveys, and faculty feedback.

Objective 1.5: Provide appropriate support for Law School library.
a. Maintain Millennium infrastructure and core data. Provide training as appropriate.
b. Work with Law School Library Dean and librarians to develop joint training and purchasing opportunities and to increase communication among us.
c. Cooperatively manage federal document depositories.
d. Facilitate use of Belk Library by law school students.

Objective 1.6: Support programs that increase international focus of campus.
a. Work with Cannon Centre to improve support of international students.
b. Provide strong online distance support for students studying abroad.
c. Expand the foreign language collection in all formats.
d. Develop displays and collections which support both the study abroad programs and the international education curricula.

Objective 1.7: Strengthen interlibrary loan program by utilizing new technologies and evaluating existing procedures and policies.
a. Implement ILLiad software.
b. Implement online delivery of journal articles.
c. Review policies, procedures and work flow. Modify as needed.
d. Analyze effectiveness of ILL automatic purchasing program.

Objective 1.8: Develop innovative public relations programs which expand awareness of Belk Library and its services.
a. Celebrate the library's 10th birthday in 2010.
b. Continue faculty/staff book discussion groups.
c. Expand display capabilities.
d. Continue and further expand celebrations such as National Library Week and Banned Book Week.
e. Collaborate with all Belk staffs to market services and resources.
f. Provide student-focused events such as Game Nights and/or mini-concerts.

Objective 1.9: Ensure appropriate planning and assessment of all aspects of library operations.
a. Review library mission and goals. Modify as needed.
b. Develop new assessment plan. Include relevant assessment done outside the library, such as the Student Services Survey, NSSE, etc.
c. Develop a modified peer and aspirant library list.
d. In preparation for SACS, review, modify, and organize all written library policies. Include statements in student, staff, and faculty handbooks.

GOAL TWO: To provide both traditional resources and innovative technologies in support of the curriculum.

Objective 2.1: Increase the number and usage of electronic resources, particularly serials and reference materials.
   a. Slowly expand e-book acquisitions. Develop vigorous PR campaign. Purchase an amazon.com Kindle reader for testing.
   b. Work with NC LIVE and Lyrasis staff to identify and acquire e-audiobooks compatible with iPods.
   c. Coordinate efforts of electronic resources and serials operations.
   d. Investigate GIS resources.
   e. Purchase electronic resources management software.
   f. Analyze audiobook collection and usage. Consider expansion/format/retention options.
   g. Implement an evaluation process for purchasing and retaining electronic resources.

Objective 2.2: Continually improve and modify library website.
   a. Implement WebFeat or another federated search engine.
   b. Redesign library home page.
   c. Create staffing solution for adequate, ongoing development and timely updating.
   d. Work with professor Rebecca Pope-Ruark and her students to implement video instructional modules on the website.

Objective 2.3: Continue and expand collaboration among IDD, Writing Center, ELITE program, Tutoring Center, Media Services, and Library staff.
   a. Develop pro-active referral protocols with Writing Center and Tutoring Center
   b. Improve cross-training of ELITE students.
   c. Develop joint teaching/learning opportunities with IDD and Instructional Technology departments.
   d. Investigate establishment of student oral presentation center in Belk Library.

Objective 2.4: Ensure that library resources are ADA accessible.
   a. Work with Coordinator of Disability Services to improve Belk facilities, resources, and services to disabled students.
   b. Ensure that the library's website is ADA compliant.
   c. Conduct "disabilities audit" of Belk Library.

Objective 2.5: Continually evaluate and update the collection to support new and changing curricula on campus.
   a. Expand and improve departmental reviews.
   b. Work with Curriculum Committee to anticipate needs of new majors, minors, courses, and programs.
   c. Expand stacks management program to ensure ease of access to traditional print resources.

GOAL THREE: To support student learning through collaboration with faculty in collection development, the design of bibliographic instruction and the development of critical, logical and creative thinking.

Objective 3.1: Expand librarian support for student research and individual classes in various and innovative ways.
   a. Develop links with the Blackboard system for appropriate library resources and for librarian support of individual courses.
   b. Provide efficient, quality access to course reserves.

   c. Ensure continued support for summer online undergraduate courses.

   d. Provide support to both students and faculty in Living/Learning Communities.

Objective 3.2: Expand liaison librarian program to increase contacts with faculty and professional staff.

   a. Analyze results of 2008 Faculty Survey and consider programmatic changes based on responses.

   b. Provide leadership in the management of copyright and intellectual property rights on campus.

   c. Increase interactions with professional departments on campus – CATL, Career Center, Academic Advising, Leadership, Student Life, Cannon Centre.

   d. Facilitate departmental library assessments during external reviews.

   e. Strengthen interactions, both in breadth and depth, between liaison librarians and their assigned departments.

Objective 3.3: Support university accreditation efforts, particularly SACS, NCATE, AACSB and ACEJMC.

   a. Provide active support to Assistant VP for Academic Affairs in preparation of SACS self study and supplemental materials.

   b. Offer statistical and research support to departments and programs preparing for accreditation.

Objective 3.4: Work with General Studies Council, Common Reading Committee and Graduate Council to provide support for meeting their goals, including those for information literacy.

   a. Participate actively in the upcoming General Studies review.

   b. Provide research support to the Common Reading Committee.

   c. Deepen involvement with Graduate Council. Request non-voting or guest membership.

GOAL FOUR: To teach effective techniques for information gathering, evaluation and presentation.

Objective 4.1: Strengthen and expand the library instruction program for students through faculty collaboration and innovative models.

   a. Develop learning outcomes for information literacy efforts.

   b. Implement new methods of assessment of effectiveness of library instruction.

   c. Expand portfolio of instruction offerings, experimenting with content, format, and delivery options.

   d. Work with Director of General Studies, Director of Elon 101, and Director of Freshman English to ensure all freshmen receive adequate library orientation.

   e. Initiate comprehensive review of services for graduate students. Implement change as appropriate.

   f. Strengthen support program for Senior Seminar and Honors students.

   g. Expand efforts to provide research instruction to SURF students.

Objective 4.2: Provide training and educational opportunities to faculty and staff in the use of library resources and services.

   a. Develop awareness of library resources and provide training opportunities for faculty and professional staff. Consider informal forums, visits to department meetings and retreats, brown bag luncheons and summer workshops.

   b. Develop occasional programs for Elon support and physical plant staff which highlight appropriate library and web resources.

   c. Survey faculty and staff on a regular basis.

GOAL FIVE: To preserve the history of Elon University and the United Church of Christ by acquiring and administering archives and special collections.

Objective 5.1: Expand access to University archives and special collections.
   a. Implement Archives Five-Year Plan (attached).

Objective 5.2: Develop guidelines and procedures for acquiring archival materials from campus offices and participate in development of a Records Management plan for the university.

GOAL SIX: To extend resources and services to area residents and visitors through the Friends of the Library.

Objective 6.1: Monitor and evaluate community use of Belk library.
   a. Monitor, and modify as necessary, user authentication software for computer access by community users.
   b. Evaluate late night visitor access.
   c. Analyze usage by area college/university students under the TALA agreement and modify provisions if necessary.

Objective 6.2: Review activities and operation of the Friends of the Elon University Library.

Objective 6.3: Work with the Office of Institutional Advancement to expand opportunities for endowed funds and memorial giving.

Objective 6.4: Continue and expand activities in support of the Alamance-Burlington School System.
   a. Provide ongoing instruction and support for The Elon Academy.
   b. Continue relationship with Cummings High School media center.

Objective 6.5: Work collaboratively with the Town of Elon and the Alamance County Public Library System to develop and support the new Elon branch library.

Franklin & Marshall College Library
Strategic Plan 2009

The Library has a long history of strategic planning, regularly reviewing the strengths, weaknesses, and opportunities of its programs and services. Our mission statement and goals provide the framework for annual or biennial selection of specific strategies and actions.

Mission Statement and Goals

The Library supports the mission of the College by providing scholarly resources vital to liberal education and by teaching the research skills necessary for lifelong learning. The Library is committed to developing knowledgeable information consumers. With this in mind, librarians and professional staff partner with faculty and students to enable effective discovery, access, evaluation and ethical use of information.

The Library will:

- provide well-equipped and comfortable spaces conducive to scholarly study, research, and the exchange of ideas;
- enable access to scholarly resources in appropriate formats to support the curriculum;
- select and preserve materials in appropriate formats that reflect the accumulated knowledge of humanity;
- instruct and guide the college community in the use and interpretation of information resources and technologies;
- maintain and preserve the history of the College and its environs through its archives;
- hire and retain a progressive and professional staff attuned to the academic needs of the college community;
- create / purchase and maintain systems to provide reliable access to information;
- continuously assess programs, services and collections;
- cooperate with appropriate departments on campus to maximize information resources and services;
- actively participate in regional and national library organizations to ensure effective service provision.

Strategies and Actions for 2009

Librarians and library staff interact every day with students, faculty and staff in unique ways. One of our purposes is to work with each person in a nonjudgmental fashion, responding to their requests, and supporting their intellectual work and growth while simultaneously guiding them in the use and interpretation of scholarly resources and technologies. The following strategies are those we plan to follow in the pursuit of this purpose.

1. Renovate interiors of Martin Library of the Sciences (MLS) and Shadek-Fackenthal Library (SFL) to meet the information needs of the contemporary F&M student.

The Library is a place for studying, collaborating, and accessing information. As the physical collections grow, more space is needed to appropriately house materials. Technological and behavioral changes in the library work and study habits of students necessitate changes in the library environment. Though small improvements have been made to our building interiors, both repair and redesign are necessary to maintain the buildings and their roles as comfortable, useful locations where students conduct research and spend time together outside of classrooms and residences. Students have the quite reasonable expectation that the libraries be safe, quiet, knowledgably staffed, attractive, and accessible *places* to study individually or in groups. Actions include:

- Implement move of offices, services and material to MLS
- Plan reuse of vacated space in SFL
- Repair furniture, and update utility infrastructure including electricity and lighting with sustainable models
- Seek Capital Campaign funds for Library renovation as part of campaign's academic focus

2. Maximize our flexibility to provide information resources required for new faculty and programs.

The priority placed on supporting new faculty and programs with information resources reflects the college's view that at its core are "teacher-scholars who work closely with students to realize their full academic potential." The Library works to provide the information resources essential to that mission, particularly in areas into which the college deems important enough to expand. Building on our record of diligent stewardship, the Library strives to meet the information resource needs of an expanding curriculum and student body during difficult economic times. Actions include:

- Accelerate a purposeful transition from paper to digital resources
- Review book, journal and e-resource budget models and assumptions
- Seek a Capital Campaign endowment to support collections

3. Deliver library services to students and faculty via their preferred technologies and venues.

As faculty and students continuously adopt new and evolving instructional and communication technologies, the Library proactively investigates, tests, and implements appropriate current delivery methods. Our users can be in the Library, elsewhere on campus, off campus locally, or anywhere in the world, and many of our services can be accessed from all these locations, on a variety of platforms and devices. Reference assistance, instruction, interlibrary loan and technological assistance are examples of what we provide on site and beyond our buildings. Actions include:

- Partner with ITS to get feedback from students and faculty on preferred technologies and venues
- Achieve the ability to offer licensed visual images and student publications to authorized users on the campus network
- Find ways to offer customized information resources to faculty and students

4. Enhance campus intellectual and community life with information resources and library programs.

While excellence in articulation, analysis, and support of a thesis may be the outwardly apparent result of the liberal arts education, information literacy lies at the foundation of that outcome. Personalized research-skills instruction, which often yields the most successful results when taught one-to-one, is a valuable complement to a successful liberal arts education program. As the college enhances programs and venues to encourage student intellectual engagement beyond the classroom these initiatives present the Library with opportunities to augment existing outreach efforts. Actions include:

- Increase one-on-one mentoring and outreach to independent study, directed reading/tutorial, and internship-for-credit students
- Seek collaborations with selected campus centers and programs
- Support the information needs of students who participate in study abroad programs
- Develop informal House liaison activities into sustainable programs and services

5. Assess programs and services, and use results to inform future strategic plans.

According to the College's Strategic Plan "an important change in the ethos of F&M has been the development of a culture of assessment across the institution..." The Library's ability to assess its own programs and services, and to demonstrate the flexibility it needs to use the results to inform future strategic plans, is key to improving, expanding, and tailoring information services. Having successfully used LibQual and other assessment tools to learn and respond to what our users think, we will continue to identify and apply useful instruments that will tell us where improvement is needed. Actions include:

- Administer LibQual+ in March 2009
- Measure information literacy efforts through National Survey of Student Engagement (NSSE) and the Research Practices Survey (RPS)
- Administer the Measuring the Impact of Networked Electronic Services (MINES) use survey in Fall 2009

Furman University Libraries Strategic Plan – August 2007

In the next five years, the library will implement the strategic goals outlined below by building on the strengths of our organizational culture. Library operations will focus on providing a user-centered experience. We will integrate emerging technologies into our culture of service. Systematic assessment of operations will assist us in adapting to a changing environment.

A. The library will maximize the effectiveness of its operations.

- Promote an organizational climate that encourages creativity, reflection, inspiration and growth.
- Foster a candid, collegial and communicative culture.
- Develop new partnerships across the library's departments.
- Evaluate and optimize workflows using internal and external resources.
- Maximize effectiveness of existing personnel by evaluating outsourcing opportunities and an increased utilization of student workers, freeing faculty and staff to pursue new projects and directions.
- Examine the library's organizational structure and adapt to emerging needs.
- Support targeted training and professional development.

B. The library will define and communicate its value.

- Improve library branding, marketing, and outreach.
- Revise the library liaison program and leverage it as a means to deliver services.
- Develop and implement information fluency instruction (IFI) for the First Year Writing seminar (FYW).
- Provide leadership in the Digicenter.
- Implement services for the new Science Library that reflect its interdisciplinary nature and the changing information landscape.

C. The library will increase the relevance of its collections.

- Implement a systematic weeding/storage strategy to optimize the use of the collections.
- Systematically assess the collections and their use.
- Build collections in the preferred formats to optimize the user experience.

D. The library will incorporate appropriate tools, technologies, and practices into its services.

- Implement a solution for more effective search and discovery of local and global resources.
- Implement a desktop delivery solution and PASCAL Delivers.
- Digitize targeted collections to improve library services.
- Reconceptualize the library's web presence.

Mount Union College

MOUNT UNION COLLEGE LIBRARY
STRATEGIC PLAN
2009 - 2012

MISSION STATEMENT:

The Mount Union College Library is an active partner in the development of information literate students, preparing them for academic success and for life in an information society.

GOAL 1: Information Literacy

Promote information literacy throughout the academic community by teaching users to find, evaluate, and make intelligent use of information resources.

1. Collaborate with faculty to create a formalized information literacy program.
2. Integrate basic information literacy competency skills into general education courses.
3. Prepare instructional sessions that support class assignments and projects.
4. Work with faculty to incorporate information literacy components into all levels of instruction in each discipline.
5. Work with other programs on campus, such as Writing across the Curriculum, First Year Experience, LS 100, Residential Life, Service Learning and the Honors Program, to incorporate information literacy standards into their programs.
6. Develop print, podcast and online tutorials to enhance students' information literacy skills.
7. Offer a college credit course in research methods and information literacy.

GOAL 2: Collection Development

Provide access to information resources in all formats, designed to support the college curriculum and the research needs of our students and faculty.

1. Revise our collection development policy to reflect the changing mix of print and electronic resources in a complex cooperative environment.
2. Build strong book collections, both print and electronic, reflecting the subject scope of our curriculum and at a research level appropriate to the needs of our users.
3. Build strong journal collections, directly supportive of our academic requirements, whenever possible in electronic full-text formats.
4. Provide reference collections and finding aids to assist in course related research.
5. Continue to make government information easily accessible by acquiring, cataloging, and delivering it in the most efficient formats.
6. Expand the collection of non-traditional academic resources, including graphic materials, digitized content and audio-visual materials.
7. Provide additional space for the expansion of the college's archival and historical collections.

October, 2008

40 - Documents - (1-5 Pages)

GOAL 3: Intellectual Environment

Create a more comfortable, safe and user friendly environment for study, research and information sharing.

1. Conduct a study of library security arrangements to determine the best way to provide a safe user environment and protect library equipment and collections.
2. Improve lighting in all areas of the library, including study spaces, stack areas and stairwells.
3. Develop an Educational Media Center which will include K-12 resources, necessary equipment for these resources, and appropriate support staff.
4. Convert existing photocopiers and computer printers to digital copier/scanners.
5. Explore the renovation of the North Reading Room for possible use as a public presentation space.
6. Replace a select number of study carrels with comfortable seating or open study tables.
7. Increase the number of group study rooms and update existing rooms with the latest technology.
8. Create and equip a group project preparation space.
9. Upgrade the old building elevator to comply with ADA standards.
10. Schedule activities within the library such as an academic speaker series, lectures, read-ins, commercial displays and book fairs.

GOAL 4: Staff Development

Recruit, develop and motivate a diverse and well-qualified staff team who can make a significant contribution to the academic mission of the college.

1. Evaluate library staffing needs and work spaces to improve the efficiency of departmental operations.
2. Provide structured orientation, library training and online tutorials for all staff members and student assistants.
3. Provide training and growth opportunities that encourage staff members to develop expertise related to their job assignments including attendance at library conferences and training sessions, participation in the governance of library cooperatives and organizations and the monitoring of current professional literature.
4. Establish fair and consistent work policies and procedures, including frequently updated job descriptions, evaluations and departmental job manuals.
5. Lobby for staff pay levels at least equivalent to state and national averages for comparable positions.

October, 2008

6. Encourage job pride, positive changes and creativity through rewards, team building exercises and off-campus retreats.
7. Improve communication among and between library staff and the rest of the campus community.

GOAL 5: Access Services

Provide user friendly access to a wide range of information resources and the support services needed to make intelligent use of these resources.

1. Organize and maintain library collections to improve access for all users, including patrons with disabilities.
2. Update and improve the library catalog, web pages and electronic resources in order to provide user friendly information retrieval service.
3. Continue to explore new methods of delivering materials to patrons in electronic formats.
4. Set fair and reasonable circulation policies that allow patrons to access materials effectively and efficiently.
5. Improve Interlibrary Loan delivery mechanisms in order to facilitate the ease of transporting resources to our users.
6. Make course materials available, either online or in print, through local collection building, course reserves, patron initiated OhioLINK circulation and interlibrary loan service.
7. Provide quality reference assistance through in-person and virtual reference services.

GOAL 6: Marketing

Promote the usage of library resources and services through a program of advertising and user education.

1. Enhance library web pages to facilitate patron access to all library services.
2. Use library displays to promote our collection strengths and unique resources.
3. Take an active part in community programs in order to increase library visibility.
4. Promote library resources and services through articles in campus publications and local newspapers.
5. Identify appropriate settings for faculty instruction in the use of library resources.
6. Ensure that the library is represented at campus activities, including job fairs and Senior Salute.
7. Produce media advertising spots promoting library resources and services for broadcast on the campus closed circuit television system and radio station.
8. Market library services, new databases and products, and the use of local and OhioLINK delivery services to the campus community.

October, 2008

GOAL 7: Digitization

Establish a program for the digitization of key documents in the history of Mount Union College and provide for their availability to all members of the College community through easy internet access.

1. Work with the OhioLINK Digitization Committee to prepare software and equipment standards to enable a campus digitization project.
2. Select and acquire scanning equipment necessary for the digitization of local collections and set aside an appropriate space for its use.
3. Hire and train staff and student assistants to conduct the digitization of key Mount Union collections.
4. Complete a trial digitization project by converting to digital form the Mount Union photograph collection housed in the library Historical Collection.
5. Work with faculty and administration to determine which collections should be digitized and set a list of priorities.
6. Encourage the appointment of a Coordinator for the Mount Union Resource Commons site and work with this coordinator to determine the structure of the site and appropriate access protocols.
7. Work with the Registrar and Department Chairs on the digitization of Senior Culminating Projects.

GOAL 8: Assessment

Develop effective procedures for the assessment of library services and facilities.

1. Develop and administer a biennial user survey, using LibQual+ or other commercial survey products, to measure user satisfaction levels and provide direction for the improvement of library facilities and services.
2. Prepare annual pre-tests and post-tests of student information literacy levels and administer them to freshmen and seniors.
3. Make use of focus groups to provide feedback and recommendations for changes in library web pages and services.
4. Collect and evaluate usage data of library web pages, databases, journal downloads and the library catalog.
5. Collect and analyze library statistical measures and compare them with statistics of similar institutions.

October, 2008

Strategic Plan
2009-2011

Shawnee State University
Clark Memorial Library

Strategic Plan 2009-2011

The mission of Clark Memorial Library is to "**bring people and information together**" to foster excellence in learning, teaching and research. To accomplish this mission we are committed to:

- contributing to the pursuit and application of knowledge through providing access and delivering quality information.
- collaborating in the pedagogy of teaching and research, and provide reference and instructional services.
- teaching users to efficiently and effectively access, evaluate and utilize information resources.
- advancing critical thinking skills, quality research instruction and intellectual diversity in order to graduate information literate, globally competitive and productive citizens.
- providing collections, services and programs to support faculty, students and staff in achieving the educational objectives of the university.
- making available the technology needed to access and utilize Clark Memorial Library and OhioLINK resources.
- providing a comfortable, accommodating environment for study and research, intellectual growth and personal development.

Goal #1: To improve the appearance and functionality of the Clark Memorial Library building to better support the needs of users.

- **Action Item #1**: Lobby to fund a remodeling plan which will include the refurbishing and/or replacement of existing furniture, new carpeting throughout the building, new group study rooms, one service counter, new equipment as needed in the Technology Assistance Center, infrastructure upgrades, etc. (Fall 2008-)

- **Action Item #2** Implement the remodeling plan as developed. (Summer 2009)

Goal #2: To work collaboratively with faculty to integrate library resources and information literacy skill into the curriculum.

- **Action Item #1**: Create an online information literacy module for introductory English classes. (Fall 2008)

- **Action Item #2**: Continue to expand and improve our information literacy program and assess its effectiveness. (Winter 2009-)

- **Action Item #3**: Action Item #3:Partner with faculty to integrate information competencies into their courses. (Fall 2008-)

- **Action Item #4**: Upgrade the circulation library position to full time. (Fall 2008)

Goal #3: Use technology to deliver resources, assist and teach users and improve the technology skills of SSU's students, faculty and staff.

- <u>Action Item #1</u>: Implement EZ Proxy to make off-campus access more transparent and improve usage statistics tabulation.

- <u>Action Item #2</u>: Improve on site reference services and implement Roaming Reference (Winter 2009)

- <u>Action Item #3</u>: Develop a Technology Assistance Center (TAC) by revamping and expanding the Curriculum Materials Center into a high-tech digital materials creation center for students and faculty. (Summer 2009)

- <u>Action Item #4</u>: Continue to revise and enrich the Library website to offer easier access to resources. (e.g. blogs, Google Scholar, simplified searching, etc.) (Fall 2008-)

- <u>Action Item #5</u>: Participate in the statewide chat/ messaging service (KIN) to allow the university community to interact electronically with a librarian. (Fall 2008-)

Goal #4: To expand access to physical and electronic library materials in support of classroom instruction and research.

- <u>Action Item #1</u>: Implement ways to allow access to resources using mobile technology (Spring 2009)

- <u>Action Item #2</u>: Enhance funding for library resources in the budget process and align with national cost levels. (Fall 2009)

- <u>Action Item #3</u>: Assure that sufficient funds are available to both purchase local resources and to participate in joint ventures with other OhioLINK libraries. (Spring 2009)

- <u>Action Item #4</u>: Acquire increased funding to support new undergraduate and graduate courses and degrees as developed (e.g. Occupational Therapy. (Spring 2009).

Goal #5: Assess the quality, relevancy, and effectiveness of its resources and services, and use assessment data to improve the collection and services.

- <u>Action Item #1</u>: To conduct user surveys annually to supplement this data. (Spring term)

Goal #6: To better publicize the services, facilities, technology, etc. that are available to the University community in support of instruction and research.

- <u>Action Item #1</u>: Finalize a marketing plan to promote services to faculty, students, staff and the community. (Fall 2008)

- <u>Action Item #2</u>: Actively promote services and resources via the library website and other means identified in the marketing plan. (Fall 2008-)

Goal #7: To continue to offer collaborative, cultural and educational programming open to the community in support of the University mission.

- <u>Action Item #1</u>: Maintain a leadership role in the "Big Read" literacy initiative as a means of enriching the community as part of the campus mission. (Spring 2009)

- <u>Action Item #2</u>: Offer other programs as funds allow to highlight and display faculty research and creative endeavors. (Spring 2009)

Shawnee State University
Clark Memorial Library

940 2nd Street,
Portsmouth, OH 45662
(740) 351.3323; library.shawnee.edu

University of Baltimore

LANGSDALE LIBRARY STRATEGIC PLAN FY 2009-2012

◎ Find It

◉ Get It

◉ Use It

◉ About Us

Hours
Directions
Floor Plans
Staff
Library Liaisons
Mission & Vision
History

◉ **Read All About It**

◉ Home

Langsdale Library promotes the mission of the University by actively supporting the teaching, learning, research, and information needs of University community members through its resources, services and instruction

INTRODUCTION

Langsdale Library continues to face the challenge of responding to rapid growth and change in technology, programs, and services. The introduction of freshmen and sophomores and the proliferation of new programs in the liberal arts create substantial challenges in meeting the needs of the UB community in the face of limited resources. The Library is committed to ongoing review of its resources and services to maximize its benefit to the University community, especially through cooperation and coordination with other departments in the University, the other University System of Maryland and Affiliated Institutions (USMAI) Libraries, and area academic libraries.

The following Library strategic initiatives and supporting objectives align closely with the University's vision statements and strategic goals. These initiatives demonstrate the library's commitment to continued support of the University overarching mission.

GOALS AND OBJECTIVES

GOAL: The Library will improve and expand its information literacy activities.

- *Objective 1*: In consultation with the Dean of the Yale Gordon College of Liberal Arts and Director of the First & Second Year program develop a five-year plan for hiring additional instruction librarian positions to teach information literacy at the first-year and transfer level by the end of FY 2009 *(UB Strategic Goal 1, Objective 1.2, Strategic Goal 6, Objective 6.5)*

- *Objective 2*: Library staff, in consultation with the faculty of the Merrick School of Business and Yale Gordon College of Liberal Arts, will annually assess its information literacy course in the University's learning communities and other information literacy instruction to determine methods for improving their effectiveness and identify gaps in students' skill sets.*(UB Strategic Goal 1, Objective 1.4)*

GOAL: The Library will provide the necessary resources and materials to support the curricular, cultural, and intellectual needs of the University community.

- *Objective 1*: The Library will design a five-year staffing plan for both librarians and staff to respond to the growth in programs and student population by the end of FY2009. *(UB Strategic Goal 1, Objective 1.5)*

- *Objective 2*: The Library staff will give priority to acquiring information in electronic and other formats that facilitate 24/7 access to resources *(UB Strategic Goal 1, Objective 1.5).*

- *Objective 3*: The Library staff will consult with faculty to determine necessary resources and services for current and new academic programs and the most effective means of providing them *(UB Strategic Goal 1, Objective 1.5).*

- *Objective 4*: The Library will develop a schedule by the end of FY2009 to regularly evaluate the collection, with all areas reviewed at least once every three years *(UB Strategic Goal 1, Objective 1.5).*

- *Objective 5*: The Library will acquire material that represents a wide variety of perspectives on research topics *(UB Strategic Goal 1, Objective 1.5).*

- *Objective 6*: The Library staff will, within budgetary limits, seek to provide resources in broad areas of intellectual and cultural interests beyond the curriculum *(UB Strategic Goal 1, Objective 1.5).*

- *Objective 7*: The Library will endeavor to purchase in the most popular formats, such as DVD, and replace material in older formats with material in new and popular formats *(UB Strategic Goal 1, Objective 1.5).*

- *Objective 8*: The Library will work closely with the University's Law Library to explore opportunities for leveraging resources and coordinate policies and activities of mutual concern *(UB Strategic Goal 1, Objective 1.5).*

- *Objective 9*: The Library will renovate Room 202 to house the Technical Services and Access Services departments by January 1, 2009, to improve working conditions and efficiency *(UB Strategic Goal 1, Objective 1.5)*

- *Objective 10*: The Library will complete its renovation of public areas to provide an attractive, usable, and safe environment for Library users by FY2011 *(UB Strategic Goal 1, Objective 1.5).*

GOAL: The Library will strengthen its service to the Baltimore region, develop ongoing relationships with local and regional organizations, and expand it resources related to the history of Baltimore and the region.

- *Objective 1*: The Library's Special Collections department will work closely with University centers, programs, and institutes, as well as other libraries and organizations, to develop community-based and interdisciplinary programs and to determine appropriate local-history materials for addition to the collection *(UB Strategic Goal 3, Objective 3.1).*
- *Objective 2*: The Library's Special Collections department will make at least 15% of its material available online by June, 2011 *(UB Strategic Goal 3, Objective 3.2).*
- *Objective 3*: The Library will improve access to these digitized collections by integrating them into its catalog, its website and other online resources *(UB Strategic Goal 3, Objective 3.2).*

GOAL: The Library will develop a marketing plan to increase the UB community's awareness of its services so that students, staff, and faculty may make use of library resources for greater student success and faculty research.

- *Objective 1*: The Library will complete an assessment of patron needs through a variety of methods (surveys, focus groups, etc) in FY09 *(UB Strategic Goal 1, Objective 1.4).*
- *Objective 2*: The Library will produce an annual marketing plan that specifies activities that will enhance the University community's awareness of Library activities and services *(UB Strategic Goal 1, Objective 1.3).*
- *Objective 3*: The Library staff will market its services and resources to ensure that the Library is integral to the intellectual life of the University *(UB Strategic Goal 1, Objective 1.3).*
- *Objective 4*: The Library will promote its activities through the use of its online newsletter, regular contact with University stakeholders, and especially the use of emerging technologies *(UB Strategic Goal 1, Objective 1.5).*

GOAL: The Library will become an intellectual commons for the University by providing in-house and virtual opportunities to share information, knowledge, and perspectives on issues of interest to the University community.

- *Objective 1*: The Library will support regular programming on trends and challenges in the area of information services *(UB Strategic Goal 4, Objective 4.2).*
- *Objective 2*: The Library will work with campus organizations to facilitate programming that informs the University community and will, when appropriate, offer technical and staff support for such activities *(UB Strategic Goal 4, Objective 4.2).*

GOAL: The Library will work with University administrators and faculty to establish a reliable funding mechanism for the Library's activities.

- *Objective 1*: The Library will provide an annual budget request to the University that identifies ongoing and anticipated funding needs and is in alignment with the Library's strategic goalsactivities *(UB Strategic Goal 4, Objective 4.1)*.
- *Objective 2*: The Library will produce at least two grant or other requests annually to be funded by organizations outside the University*activities (UB Strategic Goal 4, Objectives 4.6)*.

GOAL: The Library will foster a culture of professional growth and development for all staff.

- *Objective 1*: The Library will encourage staff to seek out and identify professional development opportunities and support their participation as financial resources permit *(UB Strategic Goal 4, Objective 4.2)*.
- *Objective 2*: The Library will support professional development and professional participation by providing flexible work schedules whenever possible *(UB Strategic Goal 4, Objective 4.2)*.
- *Objective 3*: The Library will consult with the Law Library on areas of mutual interest in the area of professional development to leverage such opportunities *(UB Strategic Goal 4, Objective 4.2)*.

8/14/07; revised 11/4/08
Approved 02/27/09

Boatwright Memorial Library

Strategic Plan 2010-2015

Mission
Boatwright Memorial Library empowers University of Richmond community members to excel in their academic, intellectual and individual pursuits by providing diverse information resources, personalized services, and creative learning spaces.
Vision
As stewards of knowledge, we will inspire growth of personal and academic potential, cultivate diversity, and foster joy in lifelong learning.
Values Collaboration Creativity Diversity Integrity Leadership Learning Service

Strategic Priorities:		
1) Spaces to inspire…	2) Resources to promote…	3) Communication and education to accelerate…
learning, innovation, connections, and discovery		

To further the goals of the Richmond Promise and to carry out our mission,
Boatwright Memorial Library adopts these

Strategic Priorities and Objectives

1) **Spaces to inspire learning, innovation, connections, and discovery**
   a. Transform space to more fully address needs of the University's students, faculty and staff
   b. Create spaces to engage the greater Richmond community
   c. Adapt to changing student learning preferences
   d. Cultivate opportunities for additional space

2) **Resources to promote learning, innovation, connections, and discovery**
   a. Align curriculum and collections
   b. Provide easy access to all collections
   c. Assure collection reflects the needs of the University's diverse and inclusive community
   d. Capitalize on potential of new technologies
   e. Support continuous development of staff knowledge and commitment to service
   f. Ensure reliable access for library users to state-of-the-art equipment
   g. Adapt services and resources to the changing needs of the University community
   h. Pursue opportunities for collaboration with internal and external partners

3) **Communication and education to accelerate learning, innovation, connections, and discovery**
   a. Strengthen information literacy of library users
   b. Communicate the opportunities offered by existing library resources and services
   c. Educate the University community on the value and potential of expanded library services and resources

May 2010

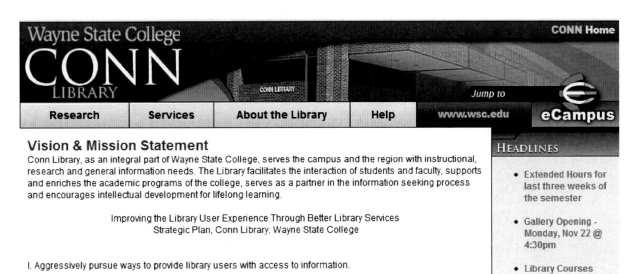

Vision & Mission Statement

Conn Library, as an integral part of Wayne State College, serves the campus and the region with instructional, research and general information needs. The Library facilitates the interaction of students and faculty, supports and enriches the academic programs of the college, serves as a partner in the information seeking process and encourages intellectual development for lifelong learning.

Improving the Library User Experience Through Better Library Services
Strategic Plan, Conn Library, Wayne State College

I. Aggressively pursue ways to provide library users with access to information.

- Maintain and improve campus-wide user outreach and education, providing opportunities for the library user community to learn information-seeking skills through concentrated library instruction. *(WSC Strat Plan – Promote Vibrant Intellectual Climate)*
- Consistently seek to improve services to actively deliver information to all users including WSC Learning Communities, Distance Education Students, and the South Sioux City campus. *(WSC Strat Plan – Increase position of WSC as regional service provider)*
- Research and implement new library services as technologies develop. *(WSC Strat Plan – Enhance Technological Infusion)*
- Work to determine needs and expectations of the user community. *(WSC Strat Plan – AQIP – Establish an institutional culture of systematic quality improvement)*
- Continually develop our educational programs to foster lifelong learning and Information Literacy. Information Literacy is defined as "an intellectual framework for understanding, finding, evaluating, and using information...through critical discernment and reasoning. Information Literacy initiates, sustains, and extends lifelong learning through abilities which may use technologies but are ultimately independent of them" (American Library Association, 2000) *(WSC Strat Plan – Promote Vibrant Intellectual Climate)*
- Support the research needs of area high school students, public libraries, and community members through a variety of outreach programs. *(WSC Strat Plan – Increase position of WSC as regional service provider)*

II. Expand, preserve and promote the library collections with a primary focus on meeting the needs of our curriculum.

- Preserve special collections to ensure access for future generations. *(WSC Strat Plan – Implement conservation/preservation)*
- Continue as active liaisons with the faculty in the materials acquisition process to keep the collection current and viable. *(WSC Strat Plan – Promote Vibrant Intellectual Climate)*
- Strive to collect materials that represent the diverse pool of writing, publishing, and producing in the world of science, literature, fine arts and human activities. *(WSC Strat Plan – Promote Vibrant Intellectual Climate)*
- Work to keep the collection viable via purchasing, organizing, withdrawing, replacing, and relocating items as necessary. *(WSC Strat Plan – Promote Vibrant Intellectual Climate)*

III. Participate in campus-wide technology development.

- Develop educational programs that will not only instruct and inform the academic community about online resources, but also enable them to use online resources successfully. *(WSC Strat Plan – Promote Vibrant Intellectual Climate)*
- Regularly evaluate the adequacy of computer hardware and automation systems, including the online catalog, public computing resources, and staff/office equipment. *(WSC Strat Plan – Enhance Technological Infusion)*
- Investigate cutting-edge technology developments in the library field. *(WSC Strat Plan – Enhance Technological Infusion)*
- Strive to protect patron privacy to the highest degree possible, for both online and in-person transactions. *(WSC Strat Plan – Provide Safety and Security)*

IV. Implement library facility improvements and participate in the over-all plan for library up-grades.

- Advocate for improved library facilities to support changing patterns of teaching and learning. Provide a variety of spaces to promote both quiet individual study as well as group learning and social interaction *(WSC Strat Plan – Continue Campus Master Plan Programs)*
- Encourage a building environment that promotes learning, is welcoming, comfortable, and secure *(WSC Strat Plan – Promote Vibrant Intellectual Climate)*
- Ensure adequate storage spaces for archival, print, audio visual, and digital collections and to provide for growth of the collection. *(WSC Strat Plan – Promote Vibrant Intellectual Climate)*
- Fulfill ADA requirements as issues are identified. *(WSC Strat Plan – Provide Safety and Security)*

V. Develop and retain knowledgeable staff.

- Continue to hold regular in-house meetings, staff development workshops and training days. *(WSC Strat Plan – Value Human Capital)*
- Encourage staff to attend national and local meetings and workshops. *(WSC Strat Plan – Value Human Capital)*
- Frequently evaluate job descriptions and work environments to reflect changing library roles. *(WSC Strat Plan – Value Human Capital)*
- Encourage open communication lines to allow for effective cooperation. *(WSC Strat Plan – Promote Effective Campus Communication)*

WSC Conn Library - 1111 Main St. - Wayne, NE 68787
CALL: (402) 375-7258   **Email:** Asklibrary@wsc.edu

Wayne State College

Buswell Memorial Library
Wheaton College
Strategic Plan

Last revision: October 2009
Lisa.Richmond@wheaton.edu

A. Fulfilling the Mission of Wheaton College

Wheaton College's stated mission is to "build the church and improve society worldwide by promoting the development of whole and effective Christians through excellence in programs of Christian higher education." This mission statement does not specify the particular forms of Christian higher education that the college offers. In practice, the undergraduate degree at Wheaton attempts to combine liberal studies with various research, professional, and applied emphases. The college's graduate degrees are professional or research oriented. Buswell Library will therefore seek to support each of these kinds of education.

1. Supporting liberal education

The meaning of *liberal education* can be understood in several ways. Most commonly it is understood as a program of study that is not pursued for its immediate relevance to a particular profession or trade but for its own intrinsic value. Such study was called liberal by the ancient Greeks because only free boys from wealthy families could afford to occupy their time in this way. Slaves and all others who needed to work to maintain themselves were not at liberty to pursue such studies. In modern times, liberal education has been interpreted as the cultivation of such virtues as liberality of spirit, sound aesthetic and moral judgments, and reasoned thought, through the study of literature, fine arts, mathematics, and other subjects. A Christian liberal education is one in which such virtues are interpreted and completed by the theological virtues of faith, hope, and charity in the light of Christian revelation. Liberal education in modern times has also been understood as the study of the foundational works and themes of one's civilization, enabling persons so educated to share a common intellectual heritage and personally appropriate its value.

As a library serving students of liberal studies, we will:
- provide adequate space and a pleasing and comfortable atmosphere in which to read, think, and write.
- collect books, essays, music, and other works that are exemplars of liberal learning, especially liberal learning in the light of Christian revelation
- offer outreach programs that seek to extend or deepen our students' appreciation and understanding of such works

2. Supporting research

Wheaton also emphasizes the development of research skills at all degree levels. Such study involves learning the norms, methods, and substance of the various disciplines in order to gain knowledge in these fields.

In order to meet curricular research needs, we will:

- build collections that can introduce students to particular fields of research and the norms and methods used in them, and interpret those fields in the light of Christian revelation
- build collections that contain the knowledge resulting from previous research and that provide necessary facts, ideas, interpretations, and sources that students need in order to carry out their own research projects
- provide catalogs, indexes, and other means of locating published research, and, to the extent under our control, the cataloging and indexing standards that lead searchers effectively to relevant materials
- provide the computer technology needed to find and use research collections
- examine course syllabi regularly to ensure that collection growth is oriented in large part toward the research assignments specified
- offer outreach programs that inform students of the collections and assistance available to them
- offer instruction programs that build students' research skills
- provide private study space in the library for PhD students
- provide extended loan periods to graduate students

3. Supporting application

It is interesting to note that according to the college's mission statement, education is not our goal but the means to our actual goal, which is "to build the church and improve society worldwide." This reveals the great importance placed at Wheaton upon applied learning. The mission statement underscores this importance by stating that "Wheaton College seeks to relate Christian liberal arts education to the needs of contemporary society."

In order to respond to this applied emphasis within the curriculum, we will:
- build collections that can introduce students to an understanding of contemporary problems in our society and around the world, particularly in the light of Christian revelation
- build collections that can help students to better understand human experience beyond their own national, ethnic, class, religious, and other groupings
- build collections that can help students to apply their learning to the needs of their churches

4. Supporting professional studies

Some of Wheaton's programs are professional in nature. Such programs train students with the skills and knowledge needed to engage in particular professions, such as teaching, music performance, and clinical psychology.

In order to meet the needs of these professional programs, we will:
- build collections that can introduce students to the norms, concerns, and practices of these professions, particularly in the light of Christian revelation

- Specific studies described under "Goals," below.

Goals

Target outreach to freshmen. Numerous research studies indicate that success in one's first year of college is critical to success in college as a whole. While the majority of our freshmen are well prepared academically and retention at Wheaton is very high, we can still assist our freshmen to make the best possible transition to college. The library will engage in outreach activities each year that particularly target freshmen. Our purpose will be to make them aware of the personal, individualized assistance that we offer.

Test possible correlation between academic achievement and formal (in-class) library instruction. Some research studies have found that formal library instruction correlates with higher-quality essays and higher academic achievement generally, while other studies have not found a correlation.[3] In the summer of 2010 the library will test the effect of library instruction by using an evaluation rubric to compare the papers in classes that received instruction with papers in classes that did not. We recognize that this will be an imperfect measure, as it will not control for other variables.

Support student engagement. Numerous studies indicate that students' engagement on campus (measured by, for example, contact with professors outside of class and involvement in campus activities) correlates with academic success. We will seek to support student engagement by encouraging the use of group-study rooms and the library café space for student-student or student-faculty interaction, holding book discussions with faculty authors, art exhibits, and providing space and support for some student-led activities.

Understand undergraduate use of print materials. The most recent Buswell data indicate that while faculty use of print collections has held steady and graduate student use has increased, undergraduate use has declined. We will seek to understand this decline better in order to develop possible library responses.

2. **Student educational satisfaction**: extent to which the library contributes to students' educational satisfaction as self-reported by students.

Goals

Conduct triennial survey. We will conduct a wide-ranging survey of student satisfaction every three years. The next survey will be held in the spring of 2011. The survey will not change or will change only slightly over the years so that we can benefit from longitudinal data. We will use the survey results to improve the library.

Provide informal opportunities for student comment. We will provide an online suggestion box on our website that will display user comments and the library's response. Our responses will be timely, written in positive language, and focused on meeting the student's need.

---

[3] Discussed in Joseph R. Matthews, *Library Assessment in Higher Education* (Westport, Conn.: Libraries Unlimited, 2007), 68-79.

5. Supporting faculty

Wheaton faculty members are expected to be good teachers, contribute to campus life, participate in faculty governance, participate in their discipline, and carry out research and personal study.

In order to support the faculty in these areas, we will:
- build collections that can help new faculty members in particular to develop their teaching and research skills and become oriented to faculty life generally
- provide private study space in the library, to the extent possible, giving priority to professors on sabbatical
- provide extended and/or flexible loan periods
- provide teaching assistants with library orientation and research skills
- maintain a strong liaison program in collection development
- work collaboratively with faculty members to provide library research instruction to students
- cooperate with Media Resources, Bookstore, Project Teacher, and other campus departments in cross-over areas that affect faculty teaching or research

B. Defining Success for Buswell Library[1]

1. **Student academic development**: evidence that the library is contributing to students' academic growth, attainment, and progress at the college.

We acknowledge that direct evidence of success in this domain is difficult to obtain. While it is indisputable that much of our students' learning would not be possible without the collections and services the library makes available, "it is nearly impossible to quantify, much less isolate, a university library's contribution" to this learning, particularly to the learning associated with liberal education. "In practice, rigor in documenting the library's contribution to campus-wide priorities is not necessarily demanded by the university. Good-faith efforts to align library operations with university priorities and to assess the library's performance with respect to [them] . . . will be appreciated despite any incompleteness and/or lack of a direct and demonstrable link between library operations and institutional outcomes."[2]

Yet we will seek to measure what we can. In addition to the impressionistic judgment of the librarians and professors, our measurement will take the following quantitative forms:
- direct count of library use, in person and remotely, as measured by turnstile counts, web site statistics, database use, circulation and interlibrary loan data, and reference and instruction activity
- comparison of library data with data from peer institutions, currently defined at Wheaton as those 25 colleges above and 25 below us in the *U.S. News & World Report* ranking. This comparative data is available biannually from the National Center for Education Statistics.

---

[1] These six factors have been adapted from Kim Cameron, "A Study of Organizational Effectiveness and Its Predictors." *Management Science* 32 (1986): 93 and Kim Cameron, "Measuring Organization Effectiveness in Institutions of Higher Education." *Administrative Science Quarterly* 23 (1978): 604-32.

[2] Elizabeth J. Wood, Rush Miller, and Amy Knapp, *Beyond Survival: Managing Academic Libraries in Transition.* (Westport, Conn.: Libraries Unlimited, 2007), 181-2.

AUM LIBRARY STRATEGIC PLAN

2010 – 2015

Introduction

The Auburn University at Montgomery has developed its Strategic Plan for the period 2010-2015. This plan was developed to align with the Auburn University at Montgomery Strategic Plan [http://www.aum.edu/uploadedFiles/Faculty_and_Staff/Chancellor/Strategic_Plan_AUM.pdf]. Specifically, we have addressed those issues of the University Strategic Plan that focus upon support for teaching and research.

The Library is faced with numerous challenges – inadequate funding, inadequate staffing, and an aging technology infrastructure within the library. In spite of these challenges, however, the library still provides strong support for faculty and student research. The library provides access to more than 70,000 journal titles via 123 separate databases.

Through the dedicated work of the library staff, the Library has revised its strategic plan to focus on three areas: distance education, user services, and technology infrastructure. Each area is integral to the effective and efficient operations of the library, both now and in the future.

We invite your comments and suggestions regarding the plan. Sincerely,

Rickey D. Best
Dean
AUM Library
rbest@aum.edu

Distance Education

Goal 1: The Library will provide services in support of distance education students and faculty, including document delivery/e-reserves, reference, and library instruction, as funding and staffing allow. (Supports Objectives 1.D.4, 1.E.2, and 1.E.3 of the Auburn Montgomery Strategic Plan).

Objectives:
1. The Library will provide document delivery and e-reserves services to distance education students and faculty, in keeping with the Library's distance education policies. (Assessment: User survey, usage statistics for document delivery and e-reserves)
2. The Library will provide Reference assistance to distance education students via instant messaging, phone and e-mail. (Assessment: User survey, reference statistics)
3. The Library will investigate the possibility of offering access to round-the-clock virtual reference services. (Assessment: Options identified, cost/benefit analysis conducted)
4. The Library will provide instruction on the use of its resources to distance education students and faculty through a variety of methods, such as online research guides, online tutorials, one-on-one consultations with librarian subject specialists via telephone or e-mail, podcasts, a synchronous classroom product, webcasts, and additional technologies as they

1

become available. (Assessment: Survey of distance education students and faculty)

Benefits: The Library will provide support for on-line, distance education courses to meet the instructional and research needs of students and faculty.

Goal 2: The Library will actively pursue improvement in its distance education services, both by regularly reviewing the effectiveness of services and policies, and by reviewing and improving the Library's Web site (Supports Objectives 1.D.4, 1.E.2, and 1.E.3 of the Auburn Montgomery Strategic Plan).

Objectives:
1. The Library will review its own distance education services and policies each year, in order to ensure that we are adequately supporting the University's commitment to support distance education via Web-based and Web-supported courses and classes. (Assessment: Reviews completed, users surveyed, changes implemented as needed)
2. The Library will continue to look for ways to improve its Web site, while observing the University's Web site guidelines. The Library Web site is the key portal to our resources and services for the entire University community, but it is particularly crucial for distance education students and faculty who do not visit the Library on a frequent basis. (Assessment: Regular reviews of the Web site by Library faculty and staff, user surveys)

Benefits: The Library will continually review and update its policies, procedures, and e-access tools to ensure efficient utilization of library resources by distance learning students and others.

Goal 3: The Library will explore creative avenues for adding to our digital collections, including Web-based informational resources that are freely accessible, electronic books, electronic reserve materials, and serials available either individually or via subscription databases, and by hiring additional librarians and staff as necessary to support the instructional needs of distance education students and faculty, as funding and staffing permit (Supports Objectives 1.D.4, 1.E.2, and 1.E.3 of the Auburn Montgomery Strategic Plan).

Objectives:
1. The Library will restore and increase funding for electronic journals, subscription databases, interlibrary loan, e-reserves, and other services and resources that are vital to distance education users. (Assessment: Regular review of the budget and the level of unmet need for electronic resources, funding restored and increased)
2. The Library will identify free Web-based informational resources that are authoritative and appropriate for the curriculum, and provide effective access to these resources via our online catalog. (Assessment: Number of free Web-based resources added to our catalog)
3. The Library will restore Technical Services staffing to previous levels or higher. (Assessment: Staffing needs evaluated and additional staff hired)
4. The Library will restore the Government Documents Librarian position. (Assessment: Librarian recruited and hired)
5. The Library will monitor the extent to which staff time is impacted by services supplied to distance education students and faculty, and if necessary, the Library will hire additional staff to ensure that we are able to meet the information needs of our patrons. (Assessment: Review of staff time conducted, recommendations made, additional staff hired if needed)

Benefits: Students in distance learning programs will benefit from the best resources available through the library in support of their educational program and their research needs.

Goal 4: The Library will explore and evaluate technological advances that have the potential to benefit distance education students and faculty, as well as our broader community of patrons, and will acquire

2

and implement technological solutions deemed to be necessary, to the extent that funding and staffing allow (Supports Objectives 1.D.4, 1.E.2, and 1.E.3 of the Auburn Montgomery Strategic Plan).

Objectives:

1. The Library will explore and evaluate the options with regard to replacing Voyager, our current ILS (integrated library system), with a new system that will lend itself better to our requirements, paying special attention to open-source products such as Evergreen, and with an eye towards planning for the major effort that the move to a new system will entail, in terms of many factors, including the logistics of handling physical items, the coordinating of technical expertise on a variety of platforms, the need to train staff, and the sheer number of staff hours required. (Assessment: Alternative systems considered, a new system selected and implemented)

2. The Library will investigate software add-on options that will permit seamless integration of e-reserves with the University's learning management system. (Assessment: Options identified, cost/benefit analysis conducted)

3. The Library will develop and implement an "Institutional Repository," a digital collection of research conducted and published by the faculty and staff members of the University that will be freely available to the campus community. The Library will be guided by members of the Research Council in the development of the IR, including collection focus.

Benefits:

By actively engaging in the University's initiative to expand its distance education offerings, and by actively seeking to improve our distance education services, the Library will gain the opportunity to demonstrate to the University that we have a unique and valuable perspective to contribute.

By moving to an open source system, the library will benefit by providing access to its holdings through an online library system at a lower cost, and with better and more frequent updates of technology, than is currently available with a dedicated ILS vendor.

By establishing an institutional repository, the library will be able to provide free access to research conducted by the university community. By working with the faculty to include their research in the institutional repository, the library will acquire copyright waivers from the publishers that will allow the preservation of digital access and use of the research without requiring a subscription to specific databases or journals.

Obstacles:

Lack of funding for maintaining adequate staffing; staff stretched thin as a result

Lack of funding for the purchase of equipment and new informational resources in all formats

Lack of funding to support the development and implementation of the institutional respository.

Student Services

Goal 5: The Library will continually strive to improve service to patrons by providing greater access to its various collections, reference assistance, and library instruction as funding and staffing allow. (University Strategic Goals: 1, 1.A., 1.C., 1.D.4., 1.F.; Goal 2, 2.B.)

Objectives: Access to Library Collections

1. The Library will work to provide accurate information for accessing its collections by:

3

       a. inventorying 20% of the collections per year for the next five years [Assessment: 20% of the collections inventoried annually]

       b. identifying problems, e.g., missing or lost books and incomplete holdings/items records, in the online catalog and correcting errors in the catalog [Assessment: catalog is cleaned up]

       c. correcting local holdings records in WorldCat [Assessment: records corrected]

2. Pull circulating materials for pick up by faculty, students, and staff to alleviate impact of cuts in hours [Assessment: number of users served and items pulled]

3. Explore issues related to self checkout of materials and implement if possible. [Assessment: issues explored and self checkout implemented if possible; statistics on items checked out and users if implemented]

4. Continue to enhance the Library's website [Assessment: feedback from user surveys]

5. Explore strategies for implementing open source software packages, e.g., Archon or Archivists Toolkit, to allow access to EAD-encoded findings aids and inventories [Assessment: software options explored]

Benefits: The library will more efficiently serve faculty in accessing monographic materials, and, via inventorying, will ensure the accuracy of library holdings. New software to ensure efficient discovery and access to library resources will benefit students, faculty, and community users.

Objectives: Interlibrary Loan

1. Utilize Illiad to its full capacity to offer services such as document delivery [Assessment: statistics for implemented Illiad functions]

2. Offer Illiad workshops for faculty and students and number of workshops offered [Assessment: statistics for number of workshops held and number of attendees]

Benefits: The addition of Illiad will improve the library's ability to request and receive materials from other academic and non-profit libraries, which will primarily benefit faculty and graduate students in the conducting of research.

Objectives: Reference Assistance

1. Implement chat reference [Assessment: chat reference statistics]

2. Provide reference assistance in residence halls and other locations outside the Library, e.g., the Learning Center [Assessment: number of times assistance is offered and number of students assisted]

Benefits: The ability to integrate librarians into areas where students congregate, and the ability to provide new mechanisms for reference, will benefit students.

Objectives: Library Instruction

1. Create short informational podcasts/tutorials with quizzes at the end, e.g., renewing books online, ILL, UB, remote log in, accessible online [Assessment: number of podcasts/tutorials created; results of quizzes]

2. Collaborate with faculty to embed librarians in courses [Assessment: number of faculty, courses, and students]

3. Work with the Writing Across the Curriculum (WAC) director and faculty to incorporate library instruction where appropriate in WAC courses [Assessment: number of courses]

4

4. Assess student learning outcomes for Library Instruction sessions, e.g., Cornerstone courses [Assessment: number of courses assessed]
5. Hire an instructional technology librarian [Assessment: librarian hired]

Benefits: Library instruction will benefit students in understanding how to locate and access information. The students will develop information literacy skills, and will benefit from learning how to renew books and to request materials from off-campus.

Collection Development

Goal 6: The Library will expand its collections contingent on funding and staffing. (University Strategic Goals: 1, 1.D.; Goal 2)

Objectives:

1. Identify areas of need, e.g., materials related to internationalization, in the existing collection and purchase materials [Assessment: increase in materials in identified areas]
2. Expand the Library's media collection for educational and entertainment purposes and pursue ways to encourage donations of DVDs [Assessment: the number of DVDs increased]
3. Investigate digital streaming rights for DVDs to incorporate into distance education courses [digital streaming rights investigated]
4. Explore grant opportunities and apply for grants to expand the collections [Assessment: grants applied for]
5. Continue to build genealogical and local history collections and pursue donations for Archives/Special Collections [Assessment: materials purchased or donated to the collection]
6. Catalog open access materials [Assessment: number cataloged]
7. Collect and catalog games for circulation to students [Assessment: games made available for check out]

Benefits: New levels and forms of information are continually created. For the library to serve its mission in supporting the teaching and research needs of the university, the library must license or otherwise acquire information for the benefit of the students and faculty.

Outreach

Goal 7: The Library will accomplish outreach activities that serve various AUM groups contingent on adequate staffing and funding through the following. (University Strategic Goals 1, 1.D.4., 1.F.; Goal 2, 2.B.)

Objectives:

1. Distance education courses [Assessment: number of courses in which the Library participates]
2. Activities and services for international students [Assessment: number of activities, services, and students]
3. Continued participation in new student orientations [Assessment: number of orientations]
4. Partnerships with units and programs, e.g., First Year Experience and Learning Comes First, under the Dean of Students [Assessment: number of programs and students]

5

5. Extend and promote traditional services, such as reference assistance, through nontraditional ways, e.g., reference chat, Facebook, Flickr, instant messaging. [Assessment: statistics for nontraditional reference assistance]

Benefits: Students will be more adapt at identifying and locating information held by the library, which will improve the quality of their research activities.

Personnel

Goal 8: The Library will maintain adequate levels of service and staffing during all hours the library is open as funding and staffing are available. (University Strategic Goals: 1)

Objectives:

1. Restore government documents librarian position [Assessment: line restored and position filled]
2. Hire librarians as needed to level that allows for appropriate coverage [Assessment: librarians hired]
3. Restore funding for part time staff [Assessment: funding restored and increase in hours worked]
4. Reinstate student assistant budget line to allow for adequate coverage [Assessment: budget line reinstated and student assistants hired]
5. Restore funding for Technical Services staff position [Assessment: funding restored and position filled]
6. Hire serials / electronic resources librarian to manage e-resources. [Assessment: budget line approved and position searched for and filled.]

Benefits: Libraries are labor intensive operations. Employees with new skill levels will enable the library to develop and implement new services that will benefit the campus community.

Space Needs

Goal 9: The Library will expand student services through better utilization of current Library space and potential additional space as funding allows. (University Strategic Goals 2, 2.B, 2.B.5.; Goal 7)

Objectives:

1. Create and/or acquire additional space for Archives/Special Collections [Assessment: space created or acquired]
2. Investigate potential space for a second computer classroom [Assessment: second classroom added]
3. Try to find additional space in the Library Tower to accommodate the print collection and prevent reduction in gathering places for students [Assessment: additional space found]
4. Explore opportunities to work with ITS to relocate a computer lab for students [Assessment: computer lab relocated]
5. Research ways to create a media production lab equipped with a scanner, color copier, and fax machine. Lab is contingent on staffing and space [Assessment: research conducted]
6. Explore options for better viewing rooms for videos/DVDs [Assessment: options explored]
7. Make better use of storage area, e.g., offices, computer classroom [Assessment: usage modified]
8. Investigate options for offsite storage for materials, e.g., National Union Catalog [Assessment: options investigated and materials stored off site if funding allows]

6

Benefits: Additional space will allow for the growth of print collections, the implementation of new technology services, and improved study space for the students.

Goal 10: The Library will strive to improve accessibility, appearance, and comfort of its facility as funding allows. (University Strategic Goals 1, 1.F.; 2.B.5.)

Objectives:

1. ADA compliant Circulation Desk [Assessment: new desk is installed)
2. Additional appropriately sized furniture and soft seating [Assessment: additional furniture purchased]
3. Features to welcome international students [Assessment: features implemented]
4. Investigate sources to provide a small number of popular newspapers and magazines available on the first floor [Assessment: newspapers and magazines made available]
5. Work with facilities to improve lighting/temperature control [Assessment: lighting and temperature control improved]
6. Repair or replace map cabinets in Government Documents [Assessment: map cabinets repaired or replaced]
7. Supply additional outlets for laptops [Assessment: outlets supplied]

Benefits:

The benefits are enhanced accessibility to the Library facility and its collections and expansion of services and collections by:

- improving accuracy of holdings both in the online catalog through an inventory of the collection and in WorldCat,
- extending services to offset the cut in hours and better serve the greater community of Library users, e.g., pulling circulating materials, self checkout of materials, chat reference, activities for international students, partnerships with units and programs, hiring librarians, staff, and students
- using existing resources to full advantage, e.g., Illiad
- expanding collections to support the curriculum and the research needs of Library users, especially in the areas of internationalization, media, and Archives/Special Collections
- extending services beyond the confines of the Library Tower, e.g., reference assistance in residence halls and other locations, embed librarians in courses
- better utilization of existing and potential additional space
- improving accessibility, appearance, and comfort via, e.g., ADA compliant Circulation Desk, additional appropriately sized comfortable seating and tables

Obstacles

Obstacles we are likely to encounter with these recommendations are:

- inability to do additional work, e.g., inventorying the collection, at existing staffing levels
- difficulty in maintaining current service levels with present staffing configuration
- lack of funding for maintaining librarian, staff, and student positions
- lack of funding for purchasing equipment
- lack of funding to provide needed training and support for library faculty and staff

Technology Strategic Plan

7

<u>Goal 11</u>: The Library will provide the necessary support to maintain its technology infrastructure needs at appropriate levels. (University Strategic Goal: 7, Obj. 7A)

Objectives:
1. Support existing services and systems for the benefit of students, faculty and staff. [Assessment: existing services maintained]
2. Maintain basic infrastructure to support future development of services. [Assessment: technology infrastructure maintained]
3. Facilitate efficient operations of library units. [Assessment: library units have adequate technological support]
4. Replace or upgrade servers owned by the Library as needed. [Assessment: servers replaced or upgraded]
5. Investigate the use of server virtualization to replace obsolete machines, avoid having to replace machines in disrepair, and to utilize our existing servers in more efficient methods. [Assessment: usefulness of virtualization is analyzed]
6. Examine ways to increase accessibility to the campus wireless network. [Assessment: wireless network access improved]

Benefits: Ensures that the library will continue to efficiently provide students with access to needed computing resources, and to ensure that those resources provide rapid access to library resources.

<u>Goal 12</u>: The Library will provide its employees with new computer workstations at regular intervals and will upgrade machines as needed. (University Strategic Goal: 7, Obj. 7A)

Objectives:
1. Reinstate the policy that library employees receive a new or upgraded computer workstation every 3 years. [Assessment: library employees' receive new computers at regular intervals]
2. Ensure that adequate funds are available to Systems and Computer Support to upgrade hardware components in library employees' computers as needed. [Assessment: library employees computers maintained]

Benefits: In order to meet the changing needs required by the Library's integrated library system, new equipment must be systematically upgraded in order for employees to work efficiently and effectively.

<u>Goal 13</u>: the Library will provide its employees with necessary software packages. (University Strategic Goal: 7, Obj. 7A)

Objective:
1. Ensure that library employees have access to software packages which are necessary to complete job duties and/or for research purposes. [Assessment: software is available to library employees]

Benefits: New software must be systematically provided and/or upgraded in order for employees to work efficiently and effectively.

<u>Goal 14</u>: The Library will work to maintain and enhance its web site. (University Strategic Goal: 1, Obj. 1.D.4)

8

64 - Documents - (6–10 Pages)

Objectives:

1. Maintain the content of the Library web site to ensure accuracy; ensure that the "look and feel" of the web site is in keeping with University standards. [Assessment: web site content and aesthetics are periodically reviewed]
2. Explore ways to enhance the Library web site to offer new services to students, faculty and staff [Assessment: recommendations reported]

Benefits: The Library website serves as the gateway to information both from on and off-campus. Improved functionality of the website maintains a sense of currency and enables the library to present a cogent message to the campus.

Goal 15: The Library will investigate and pursue the implementation of new systems and services which will allow greater access to our collections, enhance the delivery of services to faculty, staff and students, and increase the efficiency and productivity of library employees. (University Strategic Plan: Goal 7, Obj. 7A)

Objectives:

1. Explore options to replace Voyager with another ILS system. [Assessment: current ILS options reviewed, recommendations made]
2. Implement an institutional repository so that the Library can offer access to unique holdings (e.g., theses, white papers). [Assessment: institutional repository installed and accessible]
3. Explore options for making access to archival database content available [Assessment: software options are explored]
4. Explore strategies for implementing open-source software packages, e.g., Archon or Archivists Toolkit, to allow access to EAD-encoded finding aids and inventories [Assessment: software options explored, recommendations made]

Benefits: The replacement of the ILS system with an open-source system will save the library funding, and will improve access to research and development issues related to open source. Assistance with the library ILS system will be available without additional cost.

Goal 16: The Library will provide funding for training so its faculty and staff maintain current awareness of supported systems & new trends in technology. This will also allow library employees to enhance their skill sets and make better use of existing resources. (University Strategic Plan: Goal 5, Obj. 5.D.3, Obj. 5.D.5)

Objectives:

1. Encourage library employees to participate in professional development opportunities to enhance their skills and understanding of technology. [Assessment: workshops and training sessions attended]
2. Provide necessary staff training for the implementation of the new ILS. [Assessment: training is supported]

Benefits:

- Extending the technology-based services of the Library to off-campus users is especially crucial at a time when our hours have been decreased due to funding levels.

9

- Maintaining existing hardware owned by the Library will allow us to postpone replacing some equipment.

Obstacles:

- Funding levels may render the Library unable to purchase new hardware necessary to pursue new technology projects or innovations.

10

KIMBEL LIBRARY AND INSTRUCTIONAL TECHNOLOGY STRATEGIC PLAN 2009-2014

The Kimbel Library and Instructional Technology Unit of Coastal Carolina University consists of the Kimbel Library Departments (Public Services, Access Services, and Collection Management and Systems) and TEAL (Technology in Education to Advance Learning). This integrated unit provides resources and services to CCU students, faculty, and staff.

Vision Statement

As the academic heart of Coastal Carolina University, Kimbel Library and Instructional Technology is a dynamic partner for teaching and learning in a vibrant and organic space.

Mission Statement (Kimbel Library)

Kimbel Library serves as a vibrant, student-centered intellectual gathering place offering portals to information and ideas that enhance learning and research for a successful, engaging and diverse community of learners.

Strategy 1. The Kimbel Library is committed to improving the quality of and access to education through development of information and research services and resources that support student success. (Strategy 1. Goal 1.2, Goal 1.3; Strategy 2. Goal 2.2. Goal 2.3; *Supporting Strategy 3. Goal S3.1. Objective S3.1.3;* Objective S3.1.4; Goal S3.2. Objective S3.2.1, Objective S3.2.2, Objective S3.2.3, Objective S3.2.4)

Goal 1.1. The Kimbel Library will develop and manage a library collection that supports teaching and learning.

Objective 1.1. Will collaborate with faculty to build the collection with primary materials in specific areas of study to promote undergraduate-faculty research.

Objective 1.2. Will continue the process of weeding outdated and irrelevant volumes in the collection.

Objective 1.3. Will look for opportunities for shared collection development through participation with other PASCAL libraries.

Objective 1.4. Will implement a streamlined ordering process that will incorporate a faculty request system and vendor-supplied order and brief bibliographic records.

Objective 1.5. Will work towards improving quality of catalog records.

Goal 1.2. The Kimbel Library will provide improved access to the collection through use of technology.

Objective 1.1. Will increase acquisition of additional electronic resources (e-books, online databases, online journal subscriptions, etc.)

Objective 1.2. Will plan for enhancements to the library webpage and the OPAC to include newer technologies, such as federated searching, metadata, and better indexing of resources.

Objective 1.3. Will implement the Electronic Resource Management (ERM) system to provide improved access and management of the journal collection.

Objective 1.4. Will explore alternatives to current link resolver, content management and A-Z list to provide better functionality.

Objective 1.5. Will actively promote new acquisitions through improved communication between liaisons and faculty, by use of displays, and by improved visibility on library's web site

Objective 1.6. Will migrate III server and upgrade Millennium client to improve speed and reliability of modules.

Goal 1.3. Public Services will create a new model for reference services based on the changing needs of our campus community.
Objective 1.3.1. Will explore and determine feasibility for alternative models of reference service.
Objective 1.3.2. Will train student peers to provide basic levels of reference service.
Objective 1.3.3. Will implement improved reference chat service.
Objective 1.3.4. Will develop a plan to provide reference services in the learning commons.
Goal 1.4. More effective management of the reference collection will increase access and use of resources.
Objective 1.4.1. Will complete project of weeding reference collection.
Objective 1.4.2. Will purchase online reference materials as available and budget permits.
Goal 1.4. A renewed emphasis will be placed on providing services to currently underserved populations and patrons with special needs.
Objective 1.4.1. Will develop policies and procedures for students with special needs.
Objective 1.4.2. Will develop policies and procedures for distance learning.
Goal 1.5. The Kimbel Library and TEAL will serve as a resource center for copyright concerns.
Objective 1.5.1. Will develop copyright policies and procedures.

Strategy 2. The Kimbel Library will ensure that every student who graduates from Coastal Carolina University is information literate. (Strategy 2. Goal 2.2; Supporting Strategy 3. Goal S3.1. Objective S3.1.4; Goal S3.2. Objective S3.2.1, Objective S3.2.2, Objective S3.2.3, Objective S3.2.4)
Goal 2.1. Information literacy instruction will be integrated throughout the curriculum.
Objective 21.1. Will evaluate the current library instruction program using *ACRL's Information Literacy Competency Standards for Higher Education* and *Characteristics of Programs of Information Literacy that Illustrate Best Practices: A Guideline.*
Objective 21.2. Will develop a program of library instruction that allows for both face-to-face and online instruction.
Objective 2.1.3. Will explore offering credit-bearing library courses.
Goal 2.2. Library instructional materials will be provided in new formats and with better access.
Objective 2.1.3. Will explore using emerging technologies to deliver library instruction.
Objective 2.1.4. Will develop an alternative to Searchpath.
Objective 2.1.5. Will migrate the current library guides to LibGuides.

Strategy 3. The Kimbel Library will attract and retain highly qualified faculty and staff who are engaged in the profession and abreast of emerging trends and technologies in their areas of responsibility. (Strategy 3. Goal 3.1. Goal 3.2. Objective 3.2.1)
Goal 3.1. Library faculty and staff will be recognized as leaders in the profession.
Objective 3.1.1. Will initiate creative and innovative ways to improve library services.
Objective 3.1.2. Will participate in conference, workshops, and online seminars to actively engage in professional development.
Strategy 4: The Kimbel Library will provide facilities that meet patron and staff needs.

(Strategy 2. Goal 2.3. Objective 2.3.1; Goal 2.4. Objective 2.4.4; Strategy 3. Goal 3.1. Objective 3.1.2, Goal 3.3. Objective 3.3.2)

Goal 4.1. Improved work spaces will improve efficiency and service.

Objective 4.1.1. Will develop plans to re-configure the following departments: access services, public services, and collection management and systems.

Goal 4.2. The Kimbel Library will be maintained as a student-centered and student-focused facility.

Objective 4.2.1. Will make improvements to seating areas to support laptop use.

Objective 4.2.2. Will ensure that stack maintenance allows for ease of access to the collection.

Objective 4.2.3. Will plan for learning commons.

Strategy 5: The Kimbel Library will effectively market its resources and services to improve accessibility and increase awareness of the library's role in the university. (Supporting Strategy 1. Goal S1.2. Objective S1.2.1; Supporting Strategy 3. Goal S3.3)

Goal 5.1. The Kimbel Library and Instructional Technology web site will serve as a portal to resources and services.

Objective 5.1.1. Will develop and implement a new website design.

Objective 5.1.2. Will use social networking and technology to engage our community of users.

Goal 5.2. The Kimbel Library and Instructional Technology newsletter will encourage use of the resources and services available.

Objective 5.2.1. Will develop an online newsletter to be updated periodically throughout the semester.

Goal 5.3. Kimbel Library and Instructional Technology will participate in campus outreach to students, faculty, and staff.

Objective 5.3.1. Will participate in orientation and other outreach activities that promote library services and resources.

Strategy 6: The Kimbel Library will partner with the community, local, regional, and national consortia, and other stakeholders to improve its services and resources. (Strategy 1. Goal 1.5. Objective 1.5.1; Strategy 4. Goal 4.1. Objective 4.1.2)

Goal 6.1. The development of strategic partnerships will expand opportunities for service and access to resources.

Objective 6.1.1. Will continue partnership with PASCAL and other consortiums to leverage access to services and resources.

Objective 6.1.2. Will participate in SC Digital Library to preserve local and regional history and to make such information available to the public.

Objective 6.1.3. Will develop relationship with local libraries to explore opportunities for shared programming.

Strategy 7: The Kimbel Library will develop a culture of assessment in order to make informed decisions and improvements. (Supporting Strategy 2. Goal S2.1. Objective S2.1.2, Objective S2.1.3; Goal S2.2. Objective S2.2.1)

Goal 7.1. The library will use assessment effectively to improve services.

Objective 7.1.1. Will collect data necessary for IES, SC library survey, and other required reporting bodies.

Objective 7.1.2. Will collect data to support goals and objectives and make appropriate changes to improve services and resources.

Objective 7.1.3. Will position the library for the SACS self-study.

Objective 7.1.4. Will conduct the LibQual service of library customer satisfaction.

Strategy 8: The Kimbel Library will develop student workers who are competent, have a strong work ethic, and possess the relationship skills necessary to succeed in a competitive work environment. (Strategy 1. Goal 1.1. Objective 1.1.4; Strategy 2. Goal 2.2. Objective 2.2.5)

Goal 8.1. Student workers will possess the knowledge, skills, and abilities to serve the library's patrons now and to be competitive in the marketplace.

Objective 8.1.1. Will receive training in research and information skills in an environment that values and supports personal integrity, civility, and respect for others.

Objective 8.1.2. Will be given the opportunity to assume increasing responsibilities commensurate with their experience and abilities.

Mission Statement (TEAL)

The mission of Technology in Education to Advance Learning (TEAL) is to develop consulting relationships with faculty members from all academic disciplines at Coastal Carolina University to improve student learning by integrating technology in the teaching process.

Goals and Objectives 2009/2010

Strategy 1: The TEAL Center will be recognized for training and supporting faculty and staff in new and emerging technologies. (Supporting Strategy 3.Goal S3.1. Objective S3.1.3, Objective S3.1.4; Goal S3.2. Objective S3.2.1, Objective S3.2.2, Objective S3.2.4, Objective S3.2.5)

Goal 1.1: To provide training and support for faculty and staff in technologies that support teaching and learning.

Objective 1.1.1. Will collaborate with faculty to develop workshops in proved and emerging technologies

Objective 1.1.2. Will develop consultative arrangements with faculty and staff

Objective 1.1.3. Will develop a database for reporting attendance at training sessions

Objective 1.1.4. Will provide instructional materials online and in print

Objective 1.1.5. Will develop a budget for software, training resources, new licenses, and other other technology devices.

Objective 1.1.6. Will develop a checklist of faculty responsibilities when setting up an online component to their courses

Objective 1.1.7. Will provide more opportunities for consultation with faculty on instructional design and best practices

Goal 1.2. To effectively market its programs to increase use of technology

Objective 2.1.1 Will publicize in print or online faculty projects and successful use of technology in teaching and learning

Objective 2.1.2. Will use the website to effectively publicize tutorials, handouts, and other tools to instruct and assist faculty in using technology

Goal 1.3. To maintain awareness of new developments in technology

Objective 1.3.1 To participate in training sessions in new technologies in order to train others in emerging technologies

Objective 1.3.2. Will continue subscription to VTC

Objective 1.3.3. Will recommend membership in technology-focused professional organization

Strategy 2: Coastal Carolina University will provide smart classrooms, videoconferencing rooms, and other facilities that support faculty teaching with technology. (Supporting Strategy 3. Goal S3.1. S3.1.5; Goal S3.2. Objective S3.2.2)

Goal 2.1: The TEAL Center will support smart classrooms, videoconferencing, and other facilities that support faculty instruction.

Objective 2.1.1. Will provide timely support for maintenance of smart classrooms, videoconferencing rooms, and other facilities that support faculty instruction.

Objective 2.1.2. Will provide regular maintenance for classroom equipment

Objective 2.1.3. Will streamline procurement process through improved budget allocation

Strategy 3: Coastal Carolina University will be recognized for excellence in distance learning. (Strategy 1. Goal 1.1. Objective 1.1.1, Objective 1.1.4: Goal 1.3. Objective 1.3.1, Objective 1.3.2, Objective 1.3.7)

Goal 3.1. The TEAL Center will be the leader in developing communities of practice for distance learning.

Objective 3.1.1. Establish a distance learning advisory committee

Objective 3.1.2. Coordinate communication with faculty interested in distance learning

Goal 3.2: The TEAL Center will ensure quality and consistency in distance learning courses and programs through training and resource development

Objective 3.2.1. Develop resources to facilitate distance learning

Objective 3.2.2. Initiative a "boot camp" for faculty who wish focused assistance in developing distance learning

Objective 3.2.3. Develop a checklist of quality indicators for distance learning

Objective 3.2.4. Develop standards, policies, procedures, and guidelines for distance learning

Strategy 4: Faculty teaching will be enhanced through the use of the university's course management system. (Supporting Strategy 3. Goal S3.2. Objective S3.2.1)

Goal 4.1. The TEAL Center will facilitate learning through support of the university's course management system.

Objective 4.1.1. Will support Blackboard administration

Objective 4.1.2. Will use a trial system to test new upgrades to Blackboard in order to become familiar with issues and possible problems before implementation

Objective 4.1.2. Will work towards better integration between Blackboard and Datatel

Objective 4.1.3. Will implement procedures and tools to facilitate faculty self-management of Blackboard courses

Goal 4.2. The TEAL Center will explore new technologies that can be added to the course management system to enhance teaching and learning.

Objective 4.2.1. Will add Safe Assign module to Blackboard

Objective 4.2.2. Will work with faculty to make Blackboard more accessible to students with special needs

Strategy 5: Students working with the TEAL Center will become technology savvy and will receive opportunities for enhanced learning experiences. (Strategy 1. Goal 1.1. Objective 1.1.4)

Goal 5.1. TEAL students will be trained in technology and training and have opportunities to participate in training experiences.

Objective 5.1.1. Will assist faculty with technology problems

Objective 5.1.2. Will coordinate with Student Computing Services to provide basic instruction to students on Blackboard, email etiquette, basic file management, e-portfolios, etc.

Goal 5.2 Develop an internship program

Objective 5.2.1 Will work with computer science, college of education and other departments to develop internship program

Strategy 6: The TEAL Center will develop facilities that encourage faculty use of technology in teaching and that foster collaboration among faculty using emerging technologies. (Supporting Strategy 3. Goal S3.1. S3.1.5)

Goal 6.1 TEAL facilities will be designed to promote excellence in faculty teaching

Objective 6.1.1 Will develop a plan to have a dedicated space for TEAL training

Objective 6.1.2. Will develop a budget to include purchase of MAC computers to enhance training opportunities

Strategy 7: The TEAL Center will develop a culture of assessment in order to make informed decisions and improve services. (Supporting Strategy 2. Goal S2.1. Objective S2.1.2, Objective S2.1.3; Goal S2.2. Objective S2.2.1)

Goal 7.1. Continuous improvement will be encouraged based on assessment data

Objective 7.1.1. Will collect data on workshops to support program

T̲ʰ̲ᵉ̲ AMES
LIBRARY

BUILDING ON OUR STRENGTHS
STRATEGIC PLAN

MOTTO:

REFLECT TRADITION

PROMOTE SCHOLARSHIP

INSPIRE EXCELLENCE

Tʜᴇ A M E S
LIBRARY

MISSION STATEMENT

The Ames Library provides a setting conducive to interaction, consultation, study and reflection and is dedicated to serving the scholarly needs of the Illinois Wesleyan University community. Library faculty and staff develop and maintain collections that enhance the university curriculum and provide access to global information networks that assist research. They provide expertise in the management of the creation, organization, and distribution of knowledge in a changing environment. Library faculty promote information literacy by teaching the use of the tools of scholarship. In keeping with the mission of Illinois Wesleyan University, The Ames Library fosters inquiry and the pursuit of knowledge, intellectual and ethical integrity, excellence in teaching and learning, and respect for diverse points of view.

March 2004

VISION STATEMENT

As the intellectual heart of the campus, The Ames Library transforms individuals in their quest for wisdom and knowledge and the Illinois Wesleyan University community in its pursuit of excellence.

- Students trust that their needs are the library's top priority.
- Faculty eagerly seek the library as an ally in their teaching and research.
- Individuals and groups investigating new ideas and researching new fields turn to the library first for support, consultation and collaboration.
- Members of the IWU community rely on the library and its staff as a key resource for encouragement, innovation, and service in fulfilling the goals and ideals of the highest quality liberal education.
- Graduates leave the university with the realization that the library was indispensable to their academic accomplishments.

With our people, services, collections, and facilities, The Ames Library makes it easy for our users to navigate the research process and access the highest quality information resources. Motivated by our desire to understand, anticipate, and fulfill the research and information needs of our community, we continually evolve in our efforts to meet those needs. Our passion and commitment for our work inspire a zeal for inquiry in others and is central to our drive to excel. We enthusiastically reach out beyond the walls of the library, initiating and joining cooperative endeavors with others and delivering our services to individuals where they work and live.

April 2004

THEME 1 THE AMES LIBRARY IS INDISPENSABLE

Intensify efforts to realize diversity as an important principle in building our collections, creating and targeting services, and staff hiring.

- Connect with groups on campus representing diverse groups, assessing their academic needs and promoting the library
- Purchase materials in all formats to improve access to diverse perspectives
- Purchase & implement adaptive technology for students with disabilities
- Create a culture of exploration and learning about diversity in the library

Interweave information literacy into student learning and faculty development.

- Collaborate with First Year Experience
- Implement a research peer assistance program
- Initiate a research triad program
- Link services in order to assist students throughout the research and creative process
- University adopts information literacy as part of identity

Cultivate new relationships within the IWU community while continuing to expand and strengthen existing ones.

- Identify campus constituents and their research and information needs

THEME 2 LEADING BEYOND THE WALLS

Initiate and contribute to collaborative projects with faculty and IT to create seamless access to scholarly and university content.

- Work with campus groups to create and provide access to university-wide digital collections
- Serve as a Digital Institutional Repository for research projects
- Explore new ways to partner with the Information Technology Department to provide better service to our users

Deliver and distribute library services to where community members work and live, in new and innovative ways.

- Evaluate, envision, and enact changes to our reference services that transform us to meet the needs of our audience
- Enhance the delivery, distribution, and routing of items to all constituents

THEME 3

HOW DO WE "UNDERSTAND AND ANTICIPATE" (AKA BUILD ORGANIZATIONAL LEARNING CAPACITY)?

We reflect on and share our individual and collaborative expertise and experience, in order to ensure progression, enrich organizational knowledge, and strengthen community.

- Foster a sense of community among the library staff through scheduled informal social interaction (or... "Getting to know you")
- Develop a review plan for the improvement of library processes and services (or... "Why we do what we do")

We look beyond our own institution and profession, exploring other organizations and businesses for inspiration, solutions, and possibilities.

- Implement methods of pursuing cutting-edge ideas into our work habits

We pursue and evaluate data, trends and other indicators that allow us to predict changing expectations.

- Establish criteria for the evaluation of data
- Create a location for the data
- Develop questions to ask ourselves as we look beyond our walls
- Identify places to look for inspiration and ideas

We develop and invest in the fundamental resources of time, people, and tools to stimulate individual creativity and organizational innovation.

- Develop resources and a structure that provides a concise avenue for professional development within the library
- Develop and invest in a learning plan that will meet the needs of faculty and staff's professional development
- Develop and implement a plan which enhances communication skills within the library

OUTCOMES

Empower staff to translate new information into immediate action.

Evolve to match our users' ever-changing reality.

Invest in and develop a highly skilled and knowledgeable staff.

Foster an environment in which creativity and risk-taking are valued and encouraged.

Provide opportunities, resources, and a support structure to promote professional growth, retention, and advancement, thus allowing Ames to take a leadership role on campus and beyond.

8/05

Strategic Plan Timeline

Last updated: July 2009				
In Process				
Proposed				
TRANSFORMATIVE ACTIONS & INITIATIVES	Person(s) Responsible	Timeline	Target Completion Date	Notes
Theme 1: The Ames Library is indispensable				
Transformative Action: Intensify efforts to realize diversity as an important principle in building our collections, creating and targeting services, and staff hiring.				
Translate data from the LSTA study, Anthropologist in the Library: Helping Librarians Support Student Success, into action items regarding services, resources, web pages, and physical space.	Lynda Duke	2008-2010	fall 2010	
Collection Development (refine the collection development policy, develop a weeding plan, determine general policies on digital and print collections that match the mission of our institution and are sensitive to the needs of the academic disciplines; actively connect our collections to other library collections; assure routine collection management procedures are established and implemented.)	Marcia Thomas	2009-2010	fall 2010	
Transformative Action: Interweave information literacy into student learning and faculty development.				
Develop a draft version of a comprehensive information literacy program for IWU and then refine this document at the ACRL Immersion program in July 2010.	Chris Sweet	2009-2010	Fall 2010	
Create a standardized, robust, repository of info lit handouts and tutorials. These will be used during instruction sessions as well as being made available on the Ames Library website.	Chris Sweet	2010-2011	Spring 2011	
Transformative Action: Cultivate new relationships within the IWU community while continuing to expand and strengthen existing ones (proactive outreach to teaching faculty)				
Identify campus constituents and their research and information needs	Lynda Duke	2008-2010	fall 2010	
Thorpe Center: Mellon/IT/Library initiative	Suzanne Wilson; TLTR	2009-2010		
Continue to explore options for delivering information literacy continuing education for faculty and staff. Provide opportunities for teaching faculty to work on integrating information literacy into courses.	Chris Sweet	2010-?		

TRANSFORMATIVE ACTIONS & INITIATIVES	Person(s) Responsible	Timeline	Target Completion Date	Notes
Theme 2: Leading beyond the walls				
Transformative Action: Initiate and contribute to collaborative projects with faculty and IT to create seamless access to scholarly and university content.				
Develop Digital Records Management Policy	Meg Miner	2008-?		
Image as information	Stephanie Davis-Kahl, Suzanne Wilson	2009-2010		
Transformative Action: Promote environmental and sustainable practices within our library	Meg Miner, Brian Sheehan, Renee Durst	2009-2010		
Develop orientation points for new library staff and student assistants				
Create an awareness program for ourselves and our users.				
Expand and pursue partnerships that enhance campus sustainability efforts				
Adopt an environmentally responsible purchasing policy.				
Transformative Action: Deliver and distribute library services to where community members work and live, in new and innovative ways.				
Evaluate, envision, and enact changes to our reference services that transform us to meet the needs of our audience.	Sue Stroyan	2008-2010		Meebo reference chat initiated, digital reference collection growing
Student Assistants Development and Training: We devote staff and materials to provide Ames student assistants with comprehensive job training, as well as opportunities for development of individual skills and interests (Develop a standardized orientation for all new student assistants; Develop training for all student assistants on common Ames skills, as well as department-specific tasks; Develop ongoing and refresher training for returning student assistants; Train student assistants at Information Services to provide limited reference services; Strive to match student assistants' skills and interests with appropriate library projects; Review role of Training Coordinator, Training Team, and Supervisors in student training)	Karen Schmidt, Renee Durst	2009-2010		

Theme 3: Build Organizational Learning Capacity				
Transformative Action: We reflect on and share our individual and collaborative expertise and experience, in order to ensure progression, enrich organizational knowledge, and strengthen community.				
Create and implement an assessment plan	Lynda Duke	2009-2010		
Trasformative Action: We pursue and evaluate data, trends and other indicators that allow us to predict changing expectations.				
The Ames Library Faculty and Staff will 1) capture data and information, 2) organize information, and 3) share the information.	Suzanne Wilson, Marcia Thomas, Karen Schmidt, Lynda Duke	2009-2010		

OPERATIONAL

TRANSFORMATIVE ACTIONS & INITIATIVES	Person(s) Responsible	Timeline	Notes
Theme 1: The Ames Library is indispensible			
Connect with groups on campus representing diverse groups, assessing their academic needs and promoting the library	Lynda Duke	Spring 2007	
** Develop Assistive Services to Support Faculty, Staff and Students with Disabilities - Was "Purchase & implement adaptive technology for students with disabilities"	Operational	Fall 2005	Initial completion Spring 2006; on-going as population continues to change & grow
Promote the ethical use of information - copyright/plagiarism	Karen Schmidt	Fall 2007	Initial rollout completed fall 2007; ongoing refinement of message
Create a culture of exploration and learning about diversity in the library	All		
Work with libraries, campus and external organizations to create access to existing collections in a digital format	Digital Initiative Team	Spring 2005	ContentDM and Digital Commons work underway
Establish a service to build and maintain dynamic collections of digital learning materials reflecting IWU curriculum and research projects	Digital Initiative Team	Spring 2005	ContentDM and Digital Commons work underway
Theme 2: Leading Beyond the Walls			
** Enhance the delivery, distribution, and routing of items to all constituents	Operational	Fall 2005	
Foster a sense of community among the library staff through scheduled informal social interaction	Hospitality Committee	Spring 2005	
Theme 3: Build Organizational Learning Capacity			
** Implement methods of pursuing cutting edge ideas into our work habits.	Operational - Internlinkng w/Learning Plan	Spring 2005	ongoing; NITLE, CNI, EduCause; work with IT staff
** Develop resources and a structure that provides a concise avenue for professional development within the library	Operational	Spring 2005	Summer 2005
** Develop and invest in a learning plan that will meet the needs of faculty and staff's professional development	Operational	Spring 2005	Fall 2006
Develop and implement a plan which enhances communication skills within the library	Interlinking	Fall 2005	

INTRODUCTION

In spring 2007, the Missouri Western State University Library began the process of developing a new five-year plan. Library staff participated in several SWOT analysis sessions, culminating in specific library unit and individual goals. Several different exit surveys were conducted after general library instruction sessions as well as after specific topic instruction. Faculty surveys were also given after some instruction sessions.

A comparison of some aspects of the Library with peer institutions both within the state and on a national level was also made. Several Association of College and Research Libraries standards and guidelines were applied in order to assess the effectiveness of the Library.

Mission

The mission of the Library is to provide information in support of the teaching, research and related activities of students, faculty and staff.

The Library achieves this mission by

- Maximizing use of staff expertise
- Providing a well-organized, appropriately indexed and catalogued collection: digital, audiovisual and print
- Expanding access to data and electronic information resources
- Maintaining an adequate, current book collection
- Applying information and education technology in an innovative way
- Delivering appropriate, relevant information for curricular support
- Serving all clients in an equitable, timely, cost-effective manner
- Assessing and measuring services and collections against peer institutions and published standards
- Subscribing to the principles of intellectual freedom, providing access to information on all topics, without bias, toward any particular viewpoint

Vision

In the next five years, the Library anticipates and plans for

- Initiatives and goals that align with the University's strategic plan --- *Building the New American Regional University: a five year strategic plan 2007-2012*
- Clients, on and off-campus who are increasingly computer-literate and diverse
- Services that facilitate user autonomy in accessing materials outside the Library as well as on-site physical collections

- Management that promotes open communication and continuous improvement in planning and organizing tasks and that supports individual initiative and personal growth
- Staff that is knowledgeable, highly trained, adaptable and responsive, able to work together at complex tasks and to thrive on challenge and change
- Technology appropriate to meet the needs of clients and staff, aligned with the systems of the university, MOREnet and MOBIUS
- Facilities that will address space needs for Special Collections, adaptive technologies, multimedia stations, group and individual study, and an information commons
- Collaboration with local, state and national groups to enhance opportunities for information management and access

The following goals, objectives and action items support the Library mission and values and the University's *Building the New American Regional University: a five year strategic plan 2007-2012.* The Library's seven goals align with the seven opportunity areas of the University plan. References to the University plan appear in brackets after each objective. References to AQIP categories follow the brackets and are underlined.

GOAL 1: **Support graduate programs by securing appropriate resources to support applied graduate study, research and professional service**

    Objective 1.1: **Identify electronic resources applicable to graduate studies**
    [Opportunity One: 1.4] Category One

      Action item 1.1.1: Subscribe to SciFinder Scholar for the Chemistry program (Fall 2007)
      Action item 1.1.2: Subscribe to PsycArticles in support of the Human Factors and Usability Testing program (Fall 2008)
      Action item 1.1.3: Subscribe to a database such as Applied Science and Technology Complete in support of the Information Technology program (Spring 2009
      Action item 1.1.4: Investigate the need for and obtain any databases in support of the MAA degree (Fall 2009)

    Objective 1.2: **Identify other services in support of graduate programs**
    [Opportunity One: 2.2 & 2.3] Category One

      Action item 1.2.1: Develop specific web pages regarding new databases, monographs, journals, research guides and the like which are specific to graduate programs (Spring 2008 and ongoing)
      Action item 1.2.2: Survey graduate faculty to identify specific journals to support the graduate curriculum (Spring 2008 and ongoing)
      Action item 1.2.3: Gather graduate course syllabi and collaborate with graduate

faculty regarding library acquisitions (Spring 2008 and ongoing)
Action item 1.2.4: Promote graduate library resources to students on the library's blog (Begin Spring 2008 and ongoing)
Action item 1.2.5: Develop and implement patron codes and loan rules for graduate students in the circulation system (Fall 2007)

Objective 1.3: Investigate and develop a Thesis Manual in collaboration with the Graduate Council   *[Opportunity One: 2.2]*   Category One

   Action item 1.3.1: Prepare a draft thesis manual (Summer 2007)
   Action item 1.3.2: Finalize the thesis manual (Fall 2008)

 GOAL 2: Provide library services that encourage student academic achievement and faculty research pursuits

   Objective 2.1: Provide resources to implement and support information literacy and critical thinking across the curriculum *[Opportunity Two: 2.1 & 2.2]* Categories One & Six

      Action item 2.1.1: Create and distribute a bibliography of resources related to critical thinking (Spring 2008)
      Action item 2.1.2: Purchase the critical thinking component that accompanies The Opposing Viewpoints services (Fall 2007)
      Action item 2.1.3: Introduce and illustrate usage of the critical thinking component of Opposing Viewpoints to faculty (Summer 2008)
      Action item 2.1.4: Conduct a minimum of two workshops for faculty related to information literacy and its relationship to critical thinking (Summer 2010)
      Action item 2.1.5: Develop an information literacy initiative across the curriculum in collaboration with faculty and administration (Fall 2010)

   Objective 2.2: Develop new services for students which reflect their study habits: digital, mobile, independent, social and participatory
      [Opportunity Two: 1.1, 2.2, 3.1, & 3.3]   Categories One, Four & Six

      Action item 2.2.1: Create discipline specific lists of titles for the blog to promote new materials (Fall 2009)
      Action item 2.2.2: Investigate the use of "social networks", blogs, libguides, Wikis and other innovative technologies to provide library information directly to students and to promote interaction between and staff (Spring 2008 and ongoing)
      Action item 2.2.3: Create pages necessary to implement a library Facebook and My Space presence (Summer 2009)
      Action item 2.2.4: Institute the use of instant message and chat reference in communicating with students (Spring 2009)
      Action item 2.2.5: Expand the current Electronic Reserves system to include copyrighted material (Spring 2008)

Action item 2.2.6: Develop an open training component (learn & leave) for using MOBIUS interlibrary loan and document delivery services (Spring 2008)

Objective 2.3: Enhance library support mechanisms to provide a learningenvironment that supports and promotes academic excellence
[Opportunity Two: 2.2]   Categories One & Six

Action item 2.3.1: Develop expertise with metadata standards to apply tonew cataloging standards (Fall 2007 and ongoing)
Action item 2.3.2: Establish a library public relations committee (Fall 2007)
Action item 2.3.3: Use display area within the library to promotecollections and services (Ongoing)
Action item 2.3.4: Evaluate the current in-house binding process (Fall 2009)

Objective 2.4: Review and expand library holdings and electronic resources
[Opportunity Two: 3.3]   Category Six

Action item 2.4.1: Collaborate with academic departments selected for collection review each year (Ongoing)
Action item 2.4.2: Expand the collection review process to include non-print materials (Spring 2009)
Action item 2.4.3: Scan book reviews and information on newly releasedtitles to email to faculty (Spring 2008 and ongoing)
Action item 2.4.4: Seek funding to increase e-books and e-journals (Ongoing)
Action item 2.4.5: Identify and obtain additional electronic reference resources (Ongoing)
Action item 2.4.6: Evaluate current collections in line with the MOBIUS collaborative collection development initiative (Ongoing)
Action item 2.4.7: Expand library holdings and electronic access support teaching and learning (Ongoing)

Objective 2.5: Strengthen support for faculty research and creative activities
[Opportunity Two: 4.1]   Category Six

Action item 2.5.1: Collaborate with ITS and IMC to implement an electronic initiative to support faculty/student digital projects (Fall 2009)
Action item 2.5.2: Use existing and new technology to "push" content faculty desktops, IPOD's, and other devices (Spring 2009 and ongoing)

GOAL 3: Strengthen the University-wide initiative to attract, engage, and graduate a diverse student body

Objective 3.1: Evaluate and improve the first-year experience of students help achieve recruitment and retention goals *[Opportunity Three: 2.3]*   Category One

Action item 3.1.1: Participate with faculty and administrators in revamping COL101 (Ongoing)

Action item 3.1.2: Develop either through Griffon Edge or independentlyan introduction to library resources and services for all freshmen (Fall 2009)

GOAL 4: Build and enhance connections with local, regional and statewide partners

Objective 4.1: Seek partnerships with local organizations and other institutions for collection management, digitization projects, and resource sharing
[Opportunity Four: 1.6 & 3.3]   Category Nine

Action item 4.1.1: Complete initial cataloging project for the National Military Heritage Museum (Spring 2008 and ongoing)

Action item 4.1.2: Continue to assist the NMHM in developing and publicizing its resources (Summer 2008)

Action item 4.1.3: Seek additional State Library grants to continue to digitize unique Special Collections and archival materials and make them available on the web (Ongoing)

GOAL 5: Measure and assess collections, services, and operations

Objective 5.1: Continue to develop, implement, and evaluate assessment measures   *[Opportunity Five: 1.2, 1.3, & 2.2]*   Category Seven

Action item 5.1.1: Investigate library instruction assessment methods (Spring 2008)

Action item 5.1.2: Assess at least 33% of all library instruction sessions (Spring 2008 and ongoing)

Action item 5.1.3: Review and assess services against various Association of College and Research Libraries guidelines and standards for information literacy, library instruction, and other services (Spring 2008 and ongoing)

Action item 5.1.4: Incorporate ACRL Information Literacy Standards into UNV101 (Fall 2010)

Action item 5.1.5: Evaluate and restructure the Reference collection, its services and staffing patterns (Fall 2008 and ongoing)

Objective 5.2: Establish methods to assess service *[Opportunity Five: 1.2, 1.3 & 2.2]* Category Seven

Action item 5.2.1: Evaluate use of the library website through user satisfaction surveys (Fall 2008 and ongoing)

Action item 5.2.2: Create a library use survey (Spring 2008)

Action item 5.2.3: Conduct survey and analyze results (Fall 2008)

Action item 5.2.4: Conduct focus groups with students and faculty (Fall 2009)

Action item 5.2.5: Assess workflow in Technical Services to maximize productivity (Fall 2009)

:

GOAL 6: Provide a safe, supportive, and enriching environment for staff

Objective 6.1: Support, enhance productivity, and retain the staff *[Opportunity Six: 1.3 & 3.1]*   Category Four

Action item 6.1.1: Provide opportunities for each library staff member to attend a minimum of one off-campus training event or conference annually (Ongoing)
Action item 6.1.2: Restructure reference staffing patterns (Spring 2009)
Action item 6.1.3: Survey faculty to determine training needs (December 2007)
Action item 6.1.4: Determine content of faculty training session(s) conduct them (Summer 2008 and ongoing)
Action item 6.1.5: Reduce document delivery time for faculty by emailing articles to them (Spring 2008)

Objective 6.2: Protect library staff and collections   *[Opportunity Six: 2.2]*   Category Four

Action item 6.2.1: Review campus emergency procedures staff (Ongoing)
Action item 6.2.2: Develop a disaster plan for the library (Spring 2008)

GOAL 7: Continue to enhance the learning environment of the library

Objective 7.1: Improve the ease of use and of locating material *[Opportunity Seven: 1.1]*   Category One

Action item 7.1.1: Determine placement and wording of additional signage (Spring 2008)
Action item 7.1.2: Obtain and install additional signage (Summer 2008)

Objective 7.2: Improve services and equipment for students with special needs *[Opportunity Seven: 1.1]*   Categories One & Four

Action item 7.2.1: Obtain a printer for the wheelchair workstation (July 2008)
Action item 7.2.2: Obtain a wheelchair accessible instructor station for the library instruction room (Fall 2009)
Action item 7.2.3: Obtain an additional wheelchair workstation (Summer 2009)
Action item 7.2.4: Obtain an additional student wheelchair for the library instruction room (Fall 2010)

Objective 7.3: Leverage resources and provide training and services to support existing and emerging technologies in instructional andbusiness operations *[Opportunity Seven: 2.1]*   Categories Six & Eight

Action item 7.3.1: Complete training modules for teaching use evaluation of resources (Fall 2009)
Action item 7.3.2: Obtain print and electronic resources that can be purchased consortially   (Ongoing)
Action item 7.3.3: Obtain funding for an electronic resource management system (Fall 2010)

Objective 7.4: Secure increased space for library services
[Opportunity Seven: 1.1, 1.2, 3.1, & 3.4]   Categories Six & Eight

Action item 7.4.1: Transition library space from one dominated by collections to one dominated by services (Ongoing)
Action item 7.4.2: Create space for multimedia workstations (Fall 2009)
Action item 7.4.3: Create space for collaborative workstations (Fall 2010)
Action item 7.4.4: Create space for group presentation rooms (Fall 2010)
Action item 7.4.5: Create additional space for Special Collections (Fall 2010)
Action item 7.4.6: Create additional space for adaptive technologies (Fall 2010)
Action item 7.4.7: Seek Foundation support for space needs (Ongoing)
Action item 7.4.8: Secure support for naming the Library (Ongoing)

SUMMARY

The Library's unit goals align quite well with the strategic plan of the University. New initiatives such as supporting graduate programs coordinate with the existing goals of expanding both print and electronic holdings, partnering with local and state groups, and assessing and measuring Library services.

Continuing Library concerns are the acquisitions budget, space, and staffing. Particularly now with graduate programs, there must be a commitment to ongoing funding of the materials budget at appropriate, sustainable levels. Additional space is needed for multi-media scanning stations for student use within the Library. The space allocated for adaptive equipment and for the A.D.A.Technician's office needs to be augmented, yet kept within the library. Special Collections/Archives sorely needs additional space. The Library continues to support the continuation of a teaching excellence center resources room within the Library. Additional staff is needed for support of Special Collections and for more coverage at the Information Desk on third floor.

All of these needs and others yet to be identified are worthy of attention and space as this academic Library continues its metamorphosis into a living/learning engagement space............

one which we envision with additional unique spaces for student engagement, an information commons, multimedia stations, art gallery space, a theatre, and more.............an Athenaeum-like approach worthy of the *New American Regional University*.

Library Strategic Plan

Over the next five to ten years, there will be many changes in the expectations about library services, new technology and information access. For the MSU Billings Library, the areas that will present the most significant challenges fall into four major categories. Within each of these, significant goals are identified, along with actions, timelines and strategic alternatives.

Overall, the mission of the Library remains service to students and faculty together with access to needed and appropriate resources. Excellence of the Library is an important component of the two University initiatives addressing **Needs of learners** and **Faculty Excellence.**

Library Mission Statement

The Library at Montana State University-Billings is a partner in creating a dynamic, prosperous community of enlightened leaders and thoughtful, effective global citizens. The Library supports the University's drive towards meaningful education and excellent teaching, enabling individuals to achieve their full potential.

Library Vision

The Library at Montana State University-Billings will be a vital information center of the campus, working with teaching and support programs to ensure that students and faculty have timely access to the information and knowledge that they need. The Library will be guided by the following principles:

> *Libraries serve humanity;*
>
> *Respect all forms by which knowledge is communicated;*
>
> *Use technology intelligently to enhance service;*
>
> *Protect free access to knowledge;*
>
> *Honor the past and create the future.*

Between 2009 and 2019, it is anticipated that the major strategic initiatives will be:

Information Literacy

Goal 1: *Refine the LS 125 information literacy course that is now part of Academic Foundations to meet the future needs of students and to encompass changing technologies.*

Action 1.1 Examine outcomes data annually and make appropriate changes to curriculum, ensuring consistency between instructors for different sections

Action 1.2 By 2010, determine whether discipline specific LS 125 sections should be developed and work with academic programs to determine if these might be required courses. Programs in the CAHP, COB, COE and CAS should be included.

Goal 2: *Improve ongoing communications between librarians and teaching faculty.*

Action 2.1 Establish firm liaison relationships between the Library and academic departments or programs, with one librarian to be assigned to each area.

Action 2.2 Each designated librarian will meet with

department chairs and faculty on a regular schedule, and will be the primary contact to share information about new resources, instruction or events in the Library.

Action 2.3 A designated librarian will attend Undergraduate Curriculum Committee, Academic Senate, Academic Foundations and Graduate Committee meetings on a regular basis, and will report on program and other changes to the Library Director.

Goal 3: *Determine whether one time library instruction sessions are effective or should be replaced.*

Action 3.1 Between 2009 and 2014, librarians will work closely with teaching faculty to assess needs, create solutions and pilot alternative ways to orient students to the use of library resources. Evaluation instruments for both students and faculty to complete will be created.

Action 3.2 By 2012, design relevant and effective library assignments for use in a wide array of courses. Course specific outcomes will be developed for common instruction sessions.

Action 3.3 Improve the instruction workload distribution among the librarians.

Library Collections

Goal 4: *In response to student and faculty preferences, move the collection, particularly of journals and reference materials, more and more towards digital formats.*

Action 4.1 Substitute ejournal packages or digital subscriptions for print journal subscriptions. These are available to all students and faculty from any location, regardless of library hours.

Action 4.2 Evaluate use and benefits of electronic formats and reassess student and faculty preferences.

Action 4.3 Determine whether ebooks are being used effectively by students and faculty and how to balance the purchase of print vs. digital editions.

Action 4.4 Investigate and try new formats –downloadable audiobooks, podcasts, etc.

Goal 5: *Complete a collection analysis project, examining the relevance, age and scope of the Library's collection of resource materials.*

Action 5.1 A 3 year collection analysis project will start in 2009—the last broad collection examination was done in the 1980s. This will ensure that the Library's resources align with curricula of the University and will be a major responsibility of the new collection development librarian.

Action 5.2 Acquire and use tools for Action 4.1, which will include

- Reports from Library's database as to the nature, age and scope of the collection at present (this data is readily available)
- OCLC WorldCat Collection Analysis software

- Resources for College Libraries - RCLweb (lists core materials) The core list features 65,000 titles in 58 curriculum-specific subjects. Titles are selected for an academic library by more than 300 subject specialists and bibliographers.
- Input from faculty in each discipline, including new program proposals being submitted. The collection development librarian should attend UCC regularly to monitor new courses and programs.

Action 5.3 Using the data and insights gained during the collection analysis project, revise the collection development policy as needed and make informed changes to selection, deselection and collection management procedures.

Goal 6: *Improve physical access to the Library's collection for students and faculty and improve their ability to find relevant resources quickly and effectively.*

Action 6.1   By the end of 2009, install new compact shelving on the first floor of the Library, and greatly improve currently overcrowded shelves.

Action 6.2 Install PCs on first and third floors for access to catalog information close to the book stacks. Evaluate and update collection signage.

Action 6.3 Increase library space available for students in the Technology Building at the COT, with more study space and computer access than currently available.

Goal 7: *Identify and acquire funding sources for resources to support new programs and disciplines as they are created and implemented in each college.*

Action 7.1 Emphasize to the Provost, University budget committee and other appropriate groups the need to fund resources for new programs.

<u>Action 7.2</u> Add budget allocations for library and information purchases to grants whenever possible, especially those that will support new programs or new subject areas.

Student Access

Goal 8: *Improve wireless access for students in the Library.*

> <u>Action 8.1</u> By 2010, have WiFi or other open wireless access available at all locations in the Library.
>
> <u>Action 8.2</u> Enable printing in the Library from wireless access points.

Goal 9: *Simplify student access to information and other resources at MSU Billings.*

> <u>Action 9.1</u> *Work with IT, MSU Bozeman and others to institute a "one login and password" system of unified access to a variety of resources through the Library and elsewhere on campus.*

Goal 10: *Support IT in an effort to improve print management at MSU Billings.*

> <u>Action 10.1</u> Institute a change for printing over a specified minimum per semester, and for non-student library users.
>
> <u>Action 10.2</u> Allow direct printing of color images by students, with appropriate charges.

Goal 11: *Work with the Academic Support Center to offer better support to students.*

> <u>Action 11.1</u> Investigate the possibility of an ASC representative assigned to the Library as a resource person.
>
> <u>Action 11.2</u> Work with ASC to have a Library representative available as a research liaison in the ASC at specified times.

Goal 12*: Create new student study space on the first floor of the Library, using the former AV office.*

> Action 12.1 Move the Assistive Technology room into part of the former AV space, combining it with new group study space for small groups.

> Action 12.2 Investigate the possibility of 24 hour access to the new group study area, without the entire Library being open.

Goal 13: *Experiment with new technologies for students as these become available.*

> Action 13.1 Try handheld ebook readers such as the Kindle for use or checkout in the Library.

> Action 13.2 Try downloadable audiobooks or similar system in the Library.

> Action 13.3 Investigate gaming systems such as Wii in a specified area of the Library—potential gaming nights at the Library?

Goal 14: *Provide "Library Survival Information" packets to new students.*

> Action 14.1 Ensure that this information gets to all new and transfer students.

> Action 14.2 Create links from this survival information to web based tutorials and other help.

Community Library

Goal 15: *By 2013, open the shared Community Library built on the COT campus and operated jointly by the MSU Billings Library and Parmly Billings Library.*

> Action 15.1 Initial plans to be available for the legislature in 2009.

> Action 15.2 MOUs and other agreements to be created.

> Action 15.3 Work closely with Parmly Billings Library to designate optimal staffing, services, collections and other operational areas in the best possible and most efficient manner.

Jane Howell, Dec 9, 2008

Hannon Library Strategic Direction, 2008-2013

General Strategy for the Next 2-5 Years

The major focus of the Hannon Library's strategic direction over the next five years is to be an active partner in achieving the major University and Master Academic Plan initiatives of:

- Recruitment and retention,
- Learning anytime any place (LAAP),
- Emphasis on undergraduate and faculty research,
- Partnering with campus and community,
- Accrediting art, business, computer science and theatre through discipline specific associations,
- Expansion of graduate programs,

All efforts to fullfill these initiatives will be through the library's staff working to enhance on-going services, collections, and instructional programs and to develop new initiatives for both on-site students and distant learners.

Over the past five years the library has been working in many of the areas cited above and is positioned itself to extend its impact on student learning and faculty development.

The enhancement of services along with the creation of new services and collections will be clearly seen in the strategic initiatives below. The library's primary themes in achieving these initiatives will be by:

- Reaching out beyond the walls of the library to seek opportunities to partner and collaborate,
- Engaging students, faculty, and community to build and sustain working relationships,
- Creating the library has a hub for learning, and a campus focal point for social and cultural events to develop a stronger campus community,
- Using and providing instruction to new technology tools to move the library and SOU into an increased online environment.

The Library's Strategic Divisions

1. Collections
2. Access to Collections
3. Instruction
4. Public Service
5. Library as Place
6. Outreach
7. Personnel and Organization
8. Advancement

Strategic Initiatives 2008-2013

1. Collections

Division Description	Initiatives	Timeline	Team
Develop, create, maintain, organize, and preserve print, media, and digital collections.	Work with faculty and students to develop a high quality student orientated print and digital collection within a reduced budget environment. Focus on the increased emphasis of online learning and graduate programs.	On-Going	Mary Jane, Teresa, librarian subject specialist,
	Continue the move from a print based journal collection to a digital collection.	On-Going	Mary Jane, Teresa, librarian subject specialists
	Working with faculty and academic departments digitize locally developed print and artifact collections that would have heavy student use.	January, 09	Paul, Kate, Jim, Mary Jane, Deb, Librarian subject specialists
	Working with faculty and campus units create a digital archive of local scholarship, including faculty pre-prints/post prints, research from Dear Creek and Crater Lake, data sets, masters theses, capstone projects, and public information documenting the history of the University.	Summer, 09	Deb, Kate, Teresa, Jim, Mary Jane, Jules, librarian subject specialists
	Through the above initiatives explore ways to expand collections for areas targeted for accreditation. This includes Art, Business, Computer Science, and Theatre.	08-09	Mary Jane, Librarian subject specialists
Assess the Library's Collections	Analyze use statistics, develop faculty and student user surveys to determine strengths and weaknesses of the collections.		Assessment Committee

2. Access to Local and Remote Collections and Information

Division Description	Initiatives	Timeline	Team
Provide access to the library's print and digital collections, locally developed SOU scholarship, collections, and public documents, and collections beyond the Hannon Library.	Implement the following:		
	ILLIAD to improve the efficiency of Interlibrary Loan	12/01/09	Anna, Jim
	Worldcat Local to replace Summit,	12/01/09	Jim, Judy, Brent, Kate
	Expand the Electronic Reserves program.	Winter, 09	Judy
	Develop an Institutional Repository as a digital archive to house scholarly work of faculty and students and public documents of the university.	Summer, 09	Deb, Kate, Teresa, Jim, Mary Jane, Jules
	Explore if ArchivalWare, Content DM, or DigiTool should be used to store locally developed digital collections.	08-09	Deb, Kate, Teresa, Jim, Mary Jane, Jules
	Continue enhancing the library's web page and making efficient use of journal linking software.	On-Going	Emily, Librarian subject specialists, and staff
	Develop a ratio between number of library workstations and student FTE to ensure access.	08-09	Paul, Jim, Carl, Brent
	Make Special Collections more visible	Summer, 09	Mary Jane
Assess Library's Access to Information	*Analyze use statistics, and develop student and faculty surveys to determine if access to collections is efficient and effective.*		Assessment Committee

3. Instruction

Division Description	Initiatives	Timeline	Team
Provide active information, computer, and Web 2.0 literacy instructional programs to teach users how to find, evaluate, apply, present information, use social networking tools and to use critical thinking skills within the process.	Target all 300 level research courses to instruct students in discipline specific information literacy skills.	On-going	Dale and Librarian subject specialists
	Expand the current program of undergraduate and graduate information literacy to disciplines and university seminar.	On-Going	Dale and Librarian subject specialists
	Partner with CTLA and IT as appropriate to implement the three initiatives below:		
	-Develop online tutorials, video modules, distant learning classes as appropriate that could be used for on-site and distance learning classes.	08-09	Dale, Jim, Librarian Subject Specialists
	-Offer workshops on the latest Web 2.0 technologies, digital teaching/learning tools, learning objects, open courseware sources, and other information resources and strategies for faculty, students, and staff to enhance both on-site and distant learning classes.	08-09	Jim, Dale
	-Purchase and provide instruction for RefWorks and Turnitin.	08-09 or 09-10	Dale lead, Librarian subject specialist
Assess the Library's Instruction Program	Develop assessment instruments to gauge the effectiveness of the instructional program.		Assessment Committee

4. Public Services

Division Description	Initiatives	Timeline	Team
Provide a high quality service ethic to assist students, faculty, and staff. **Develop services that engage students and builds relationships with library staff**			
	Provide a welcoming and friendly on-site and online environment where users feel free to ask questions, and use library services and collections.	On-Going	Entire Staff
	Explore merging ITC and Reference to create a more robust staffing environment to help students.	Fall, Winter, 09	Staff
	Provide a positive user-centered instructional service orientation in every exchange between library staff and users.		Entire Staff
	Continue the online 24/7 chat reference and expand service as needed.		Connie
	Provide one-on-one support for technology and Web 2.0 questions in a Learning Commons environment.		Reference desk staff
	Lease new photocopy machines	Winter, 09	Paul
	Initiate a library student mentor program.	Summer, 09	
Assess the Library's Public Services	Analyze use statistics, and conduct user surveys to determine the success of public services.		Assessment Committee

5. Library as Place

Division Description	Initiatives	Timeline	Team
Provide a welcoming and engaging learning environment conducive to inquiry, research, tutoring, mentoring, and advising, and serve as a social and cultural focal point for the University.	Partner with Student Affairs to explore the feasibility of creating a Learning Commons in the library so students have a single point for academic assistance.	08-09	Paul, Connie, Dale
	Working with the campus advising committee transition and train selected librarians to be academic advisors.	Spring, 09	Librarians
	Develop stimulating displays and exhibits that engage students	Winter, 09	Staff, Students, Librarians
	Working with performing art programs schedule concerts, plays, movies, and other campus-wide events in the library		
	Implement a News Center to be a focal point for worldwide news.	Spring, 09	Paul, Carl, Jim
	Explore if all or part of SOAR could be held in the library.	Fall, 08	SOAR Committee
	Make greater use of the Meese patio by placing patio furniture umbrellas or other shading devices that encourages study and events.	On-Going	Paul, Events Planning Team
	Display all the flags of the world to reflect an international perspective	Spring, 09	
	Place art tracks throughout the library to display library art and work of students and faculty.	Spring, 09	Paul, Teresa
Assess the Library as Place projects	Assess how faculty and students use the library and if they their use is successful.	Spring, 09	Assessment Committee

6. Outreach to the Campus and the Community

Division Description	Initiatives	Timeline	Team
Reach out beyond the walls of the library to work collaboratively with students, faculty, staff, and community in promoting and partnering to provide services, collections, and events	Expand library subject specialist and teaching faculty contact to develop collaborative projects on creating local digital collections, developing the Institutional Repository, and for faculty development projects through the library's instructional program	Spring, 09	Librarian subject specialists
	Meet with individual and small faculty groups.	On-Going	Librarians
	Sponsor an event for new faculty each fall.	Fall, 09	
	Meet with students through Student Government organizations, clubs, and athletic teams to determine how the library could assist and partner with them.	On-Going	Librarians
	Create a Student Library Advisory Committee to advise the library Dean.	Winter, 09	Paul
	Submit articles to the student newspaper, send campus-wide Email, and post announcements of library events throughout the library and the campus.	On-Going	Publicity Committee
	Explore the possibilities of local businesses sponsoring activities and events in the library.		
	Develop surveys to gauge how successful the library's outreach efforts have been.		Assessment Committee

Assess Outreach Activities			

7. Personnel and Organization

Division Description	Initiatives	Timeline	Team
Develop a results-based team learning organization.			
	Continue to develop a positive and affirming team environment dedicated to high quality service to our students and faculty.	On-Going	
	Identify new skills needed by the staff to achieve the initiatives in this document and provide staff with time and opportunities during a time of budget restraints to learn these skills and methods to advance the mission and goals of the library.	On-Going	
	Monitor the progress on all strategic initiatives in this document so all library staff and University can see the results of the plan.	On-Going	
	Codify the compilation, recording, and use of statistics.	Winter, 09	Library Staff
Assess the library as a results-based learning organization	Identify the projects and services completed and implemented over the past year. Document new skills gained by the staff over the past year.		Assessment Committee

8.Library Advancement

Division Description	Initiatives	Timeline	Team
Develop Funding Projects that Advance the Library's Mission			
	Develop a Library Advancement Case Statement.	Spring 09	Paul
	Develop a comprehensive library advancement packet for the Vice-President of Advancement to assist in identifying potential strategies and sources for fund rasiing.	Fall, 09	Paul
	Work with the Vice-President of Advancement to:	Spring, 09	Paul
	-Implement the Founders Book Club	Winter, 09	Paul
	-Re-establish Hannon Library naming opportunities where the library receives a portion of the funding.	Winter, 09	Paul
	-Implement a collections endowment program	Spring, 09	Paul
	-Attend meetings of various community groups to advance the library and the University.	Winter, 09	Paul
	-Contact local potential donors	On-Going	Paul

KRAEMER FAMILY LIBRARY
MISSION AND GOALS
FY 2010
June 24, 2009 (Revised)

The Kraemer Family Library's mission is to provide information services, sources, and instructional support services that are essential to the teaching, research, and service mission of the University of Colorado at Colorado Springs. To accomplish this mission, the library has the following goals and responsibilities:

Goal 1:   Provide a comprehensive instructional program that empowers students, faculty and staff to obtain information literacy skills needed to become self-sufficient in finding, selecting, evaluating and using information.

Core Strategies:

- Establish a comprehensive, integrated and systematic information literacy program plan for students that is predicated on a progression through skill sets in order to graduate students with information literacy competencies.
- Establish an evaluation and assessment plan for the information literacy program.
- Provide students, staff and faculty with a full range of opportunities, formal and informal, for information literacy education.
- Collaborate with teaching faculty and campus departments to incorporate information literacy into the curriculum and student support efforts.

FY 10 Actions:

- Increase the total overall number of library instruction sessions offered by focusing additional efforts on discipline specific sessions. (LIBS)
- Develop a database for collecting, recording, and reporting instructional statistics. (SB, DH)
- Market and conduct at least 3 general instruction workshops a semester and at least 3 on more specialized topics. (LIBS)
- Continue working with Writing Program to include standard and consistent library instruction (LiONiL plus in-class session) in all sections. (SB,LIBS)
- Revise and update Information Literacy plan and web page. (SB)
- Collaborate with faculty to incorporate information literacy into the curriculum and assessment programs of their discipline. (LIBS)
- Seek to provide library instruction to each section of freshman seminar. (LIBS)
- Continue to revise SpLINT and LiONil tutorials. (SB,MBC)
- Begin development of online video tutorials for library instruction purposes. (TF,LIBS)

University of Colorado at Colorado Springs

Goal 2: **Actively foster a user-focused environment committed to identifying, delivering and promoting information services that meet or exceed user expectations.**

Core Strategies:
- Offer quality customer service at all service points.
- Focus on involving faculty in the library and its services.
- Provide an ongoing assessment of services and their impact on our users, monitoring and responding to changing user expectations.
- Evaluate existing reference services and explore alternative means of delivery.
- Expand outreach efforts and library programming to promote the use of the collections and services of the library as an integral part of the campus learning and research activities.
- Establish a coherent, consistent library marketing program that focuses on new and existing services and collections.

FY 10 Actions:
- Process 90% of all ILL requests within 24 hours of receipt. (ILL)
- Provide welcoming, efficient service to all patrons at both circulation desks. (Circ)
- Keep shelving backlogs to a minimum by regular monitoring of student employee shelving activity. (Circ)
- Pull Prospector requests from other libraries multiple times daily to ensure faster delivery time. (Circ)
- Process Prospector items immediately upon delivery to circulation, to ensure faster delivery to UCCS patrons. (Circ)
- Provide and market scholarly and intellectually stimulating programs each semester for the campus community. (TS,Volunteer)
- Continue to highlight faculty publications on the Library's web page. (CM,TF)
- Contact all faculty members in respective departments at least once a semester regarding library services, instruction, collection development and database availability and use. (LIBS)
- Participate in new faculty orientation and meet individually with all new faculty in respective departments during fall semester. (LIBS)
- Conduct a user survey of Reference services. (CM,LIBS)
- Continue development and use of REFSTATS. (DH, TF, LIBS)
- Develop a methodology for reference librarian peer review evaluation using data in REFSTATS. (CM,LIBS)
- Explore and implement alternative reference services such as instant messaging or chat. (CM, DH, LIBS)
- Consider alternate staffing options for the Reference Desk (i.e. use of classified staff, alternate scheduling of time periods, etc.). (CM, LIBS)
- Explore with IT the possibility of combining Reference and Computer Assistance Desks. (Ref, Circ)

- Transition to reduced student assistant budget in CIRC with minimal services impacts. (Circ)
- Review policies and procedures for distance education students in order to improve service. (Circ, ILL, LIBS)
- Promote campus and community awareness of Archives services and the contents of the archives collection including exploring possibilities for creating an improved web presence for the Archives. (MR, MBC)
- Reinvent the Kraemer Chronicle. (TS,SB)
- Continue to produce and manage the Undergraduate Research Journal by actively marketing the service, soliciting additional publications, and publishing issues on a regular basis. (TF, LIBS)

Goal 3:   **Select and acquire collections of print, non-print and electronic library resources with a diversity of perspectives supportive of the teaching and learning programs, and the research programs of UCCS.**

Core Strategies:

- Select and provide information resources that enhance collection depth and strengths across the curriculum and research areas and match the ongoing and emerging needs of the faculty, staff and students.
- Monitor and evaluate the use of the collections.
- Maintain a strong liaison program with the academic departments and seek systematic input from Faculty on selection and de-selection decisions.
- Continue the effort to build the UCCS Archives.
- Continuously monitor and evaluate suppliers of print, non-print, and electronic resources to assure optimum expenditure of library budgets and staff resources.
- Document and determine final disposition of gift materials received in a timely manner.

FY 10 Actions:

- Develop guidelines and strategy for adding new serial titles and selecting new electronic resources. (RH, LIBS)
- Develop policy and procedure for review and deselection of materials that incorporates procedures currently used by cataloging. (LIBS, Cataloging)
- Identify additional print subscriptions that can be changed to electronic prior to 2010 renewal and process the renewal. (RK, MT, RH)
- Continue to evaluate existing journals and electronic resources in terms of usage, cost, document delivery demand and value to the user, canceling and adding as needed and possible.(RH,LIBS)
- Review and revise license agreements for electronic resources as necessary. (RH,MT)
- Send at least two shipments of discarded gift books to B-Logistics services in FY10. (JC)

- Explore options for disposal of gift books without ISBN's and investigate other services such as Better World Books as an alternative to B-Logistics. (JC)
- Continue to work on the review and disposal of the gift backlog in the library store room. (JC,LIBS)
- Collect materials appropriate for inclusion in the UCCS archives including developing a plan or system for capturing email correspondence that is appropriate for the Archives collection. (MR, MBC)
- Develop a procedure for the systematic review and replacement or withdrawal of lost, lost and paid, and missing items as staff time and budget allow. (RH, JC, MBC, GM)

Goal 4: **Organize, maintain and preserve the print, non-print and electronic UCCS library collections and provide access to them and the wider world of information through state of the art technology.**

Core Strategies:
- Provide a current, comprehensive and easy to use web page that provides users with access to catalogs, services, policies and information about the library.
- Manage, maintain and effectively utilize the III online library system to maximize efficiency and use of the library.
- Catalog and organize print, non-print and electronic collections to enhance access and use.
- Maintain and preserve the print and non-print collections.

FY10 Actions:
- Establish a working group to explore digitization possibilities and draft digitization policies and procedures in conjunction with plans for implementation and utilization of the Alliance Digital Repository. (TS, Working Group)
- Continue to upgrade OCLC Connexion client software as new releases become available, and maintain currency in use of all applicable features provided by the software. (MBC,GM,JC,RK,SH)
- Expand use of III cataloging, catalog maintenance and processing features. (MBC,GM)
- Evaluate the Library website for enhanced usability and accessibility. (TF)
- Update to the new Web Content Management System when it becomes available and train librarians in its use. (TF, SH, LIBS)
- Continue to add information on selected electronic resources to the catalog. (RH, MBC, MT)
- Continue to work on the backlog of documents requiring cataloging and restart the Colorado documents retrospective cataloging project. (RK, MBC, RH)
- Address range of issues related to federal documents: depository status, closing shelf list, conversion of print to electronic, weeding of collections, cataloging of electronic documents, etc. (RH, RK, MBC, JRJ)

- Evaluate archives physical processing procedures, ensure that a plan is in place for proper storage of and ease of access to materials, and continue to work on eliminating the backlog of archival materials. (MR, MBC)
- Update the library's WebPAC interface. (SH)
- Maintain the book stacks by shelf reading, shifting and re-labeling as necessary. (Circ, Vol)
- Install new software releases and implement new or previously unused features of the III system as appropriate. (SH, RH, All)
- Monitor the release and development of electronic products that enhance access to collections including additional III modules and products from other vendors. (TS, RH, CM)
- Add information to III about electronic journal subscriptions and electronic with print journal titles, and create better documentation, especially for payment and renewal information, for other electronic resources.(RH, MT)
- Monitor and update as necessary holdings in the Serials Solutions list and explore and implement additional features of the Serials Solutions product as they become available. (MT,TF)
- Continue to explore possibilities for creating finding aids and other user access tools for Archives. (MR, MBC)
- Explore and address III loader issues. (MBC,RH,SH)
- Explore III capabilities for better identification and access to in process and new materials, specifically those on the new books shelf. (Tech Services, CM, DH)
- Train liaison librarians in the use of III listing facilities (create lists). (SH,RH)
- Expand the hold function in the webpac to include available materials. (DH,SH, CM)
- Develop more consistent procedures for searching for lost materials. (CP)
- Identify materials in the reference collection that can be moved to bound periodicals or main collection. (CM, LIBS)
- Determine options for making DVD/video collections more accessible. (DH, CM, Cataloging)
- Review Special Collections designation and location of materials. (CM, Tech Services)
- Review and revise ILL documentation on the library website. (ILL)
- Upgrade ILLiad to latest version and train appropriate staff. (ILL, SH)
- Explore possibilities for targeting key archives documents/photographs that can be scanned and made more accessible via the web, III catalog, or ADR. (MR, MBC)
- Establish consistent procedures for adding records for ebooks to the catalog and add records as new collections or titles are acquired. (MBC, RH)
- Change current procedures and codes so that order records are added to Prospector. (JC, RH, MBC)
- Address the various issues with regard to the Springer ebook collection – catalog records, marketing, copy on demand, ILL through Prospector, etc. (RH,MBC,ILL, LIBS)

- Explore the possibility of using Gold Rush as an ERM or possible replacement for Serials Solutions. (RH,MT)
- Continue to monitor developments with WorldCat Local and consider how best to implement at Kraemer Library. (LIBS)

Goal 5: **Recruit and develop a diverse, self-directed library staff team that is committed to achieving the mission of the library and the university.**

Core Strategies:
- Evaluate staffing patterns for all library staff (including student employees and volunteers) in light of changing goals, services and operational demands, increasing or reassigning staff as needed.
- Evaluate, reward and recognize staff and faculty performance in accordance with library, university and state personnel policies and practices.
- Support and encourage professional development through in-house, on-campus, and off campus programs.
- Fill all vacant and new positions promptly with qualified, technologically experienced, diverse, self-directed and self-reliant individuals who are committed to service.
- Ensure that each staff member accepts his/her responsibility for analyzing what skills they need to develop to better contribute to the mission of the library.
- Increase library staff knowledge and understanding of available electronic resources.

FY10 Actions:
- Provide orientation and training for all student employees and encourage them to participate in training opportunities provided by Student Employment. (All)
- Do annual performance planning and evaluation tasks as required. (Supervisors)
- Complete conversion of circulation documentation and training materials to online format. (KJ)
- Explore ways to streamline and improve communication among all library personnel including further implementation of the library intranet.(All)
- Conduct comprehensive review for Mariyam Thohira. (TS, Committees)
- Train new Archives library technician. (MBC, MR)
- Implement new criteria for reappointment, promotion and tenure. (TS, LIBS)
- Encourage and support tenure track faculty in their research efforts and facilitate participation at professional conferences. (TS)
- Work toward achieving the action items identified in the Library Diversity Plan and document activities during the year that address the actions. (All)
- Continue to support campus sustainability activities such as recycling, energy saving, etc. and implement recommendations from the Campus Sustainability Office as appropriate. (All)
- Participate in at least one job development activity per year. (All)

- Reward outstanding achievement with Kudos, Outstanding Service Award, etc. (All)
- Consider options for filling vacancy created by Judith Rice-Jones retirement in January. (TS, All)
- Provide customer service training for circulation student assistants and staff. (Circ, JB)
- Develop policies and procedures for managing community service volunteers in Circulation. (CP,CM)
- Implement more cross training for circulation staff. (Circ, DH)

Goal 6:   Provide and maintain a library facility and infrastructure which is conducive to scholarship, research, and serious study; and which meets user, collection, and staff needs.

Core Strategies:
- Seek to make all aware of the library as "place" by making the library a venue for a variety of intellectual and cultural pursuits.
- Ensure that facilities are comfortable for study and encourage and optimize the use of library services and collections.
- Identify and implement changes in facilities to meet library programmatic needs.
- Evaluate the utilization of existing library spaces balancing the use of space for services, staffing, studying and collections.
- Maintain and update equipment, inventory and infrastructure.

FY10 Actions:
- Provide physical and online maps of stack layout on 3rd floor and keep them updated as shifts occur. (Circ, DH)
- Reexamine plans for compact shelving including evaluation and possible repurposing of space on 2nd floor (current periodical shelving, reference shelving, repositioning Reference Desk, etc). (TS,CM,RH, JL)
- Shift current periodicals to reduce shelving and take into consideration reduction in print subscriptions. (RK)
- Evaluate possibilities of repurposing copy room space. (TS, JL, CM, RH)
- Explore options that address the need for better restroom signage on both floors. (CM, all)
- Upgrade computers on a regular schedule and continue to train staff in their use. (SH,JL,IT)
- Provide displays on regular basis on timely topics. (CM,JRJ)
- Provide archival displays on topics of campus history. (MR)
- Work with IT to return EPC239 to a space primarily for instruction purposes after the renovation of the Science building is completed.
- Pursue issues with temperature, humidity, lighting and climate control in the Library building as they occur. (TS,JL,All)

- Investigate additional ways to display faculty scholarship and creative work. (TS,JRJ)

Goal 7:   **Manage, administer, and expand the library's resources effectively and efficiently and foster cooperation and economies in the provision of information services through local, state and national partnerships.**

Core Strategies:
- Demonstrate accountability for the library's resources.
- Capitalize on opportunities to leverage resources through new organizational structures, collaboration with others, and effective use of existing resources.
- Maintain and implement a planning process with broad input that incorporates the campus planning and that evaluates progress.
- Create and implement a development strategy to pursue opportunities for external funding for long-term enhancement of library resources.
- Cultivate, steward and appropriately recognize the donors to the library.
- Participate in state, local and national resource sharing efforts.

FY 10 Actions:
- Apply for grants and other alternative funding mechanisms. (TS,LIBS)
- Determine future directions for expanding gift donor base and further cultivation of existing donors. (TS,JL)
- Reexamine policies for adding donors to recognition wall. (TS,JL)
- Submit SABR budget reports. (TS,JL,RH)
- Continue to spend all available funds efficiently and effectively. (TS,RH,JL,JC,CM,LIBS)
- Implement changes in the finance, ACARD and other CU administrative systems as they become available. (JL,RH,JC)
- Continue to review and revise method of collecting, maintaining, and reporting electronic use statistics. (MT)
- Continue to participate in Prospector and other consortia activities at the state level. (All)
- Continue to implement services and participate in activities as a full member of the Colorado Alliance of Research Libraries. (All)
- Maintain a current planning document. (RH,CM,JC,DP,All)
- Continue to work with other CU campus libraries on consortial agreements. (RH,MT)
- Develop a plan for active participation in the Alliance Digital Repository. (TS,All)
- Investigate participation in the COKAMO courier delivery service for ILL. (ILL)
- Develop policies and procedures for more effective management of ILL overdues and invoices. (ILL)

- Consider creating a new fee-based category of public patron with access to Prospector. (CM,DH)
- Ensure that addresses with vendors, agencies, etc. are changed from the P.O. Box to the street address and that phone numbers are changed from the 262 prefix to the 255 prefix. (All)
- Implement new funding policy for travel. (TS,JL,All)
- Monitor development with the CU Digital Library. (TS)

Goal 8:   Establish partnerships and collaborate with campus units in the coordination of information management, services, and literacy, and actively participate in and support other campus initiatives.

Core Strategies:
- Participate in campus initiatives by serving on and contributing to campus committees.
- Participate in campus planning efforts.
- Contribute to accreditation and program review processes.
- Work cooperatively with the Information Technology Services Department.
- Tie library instruction into campus goals for student retention

FY10 Actions:
- Work with IT on an ongoing basis to resolve issues that develop with the information commons. (User Services)
- Work with facilities to implement changes in existing lighting system. (TS,CM,JL)
- Participate with the campus in the development and implementation of recruitment and retention plans. (All)
- Prepare and submit library information for departments or colleges undergoing program review or accreditation in FY 10. (RH,LIBS)
- Participate in campus activities such as Club Fair, Career Fair, Health Fair, Graduate School Open House, Freshman Seminar, orientations for staff, faculty, and students, etc. to support the activities and promote the library's services. (All)
- Encourage library faculty and staff to actively participate in campus governance efforts. (All)
- Work with the Graduate School to investigate electronic theses and dissertations. (RH)

Widener University

GOAL 1 : Information Literacy and Education—To develop activities promoting excellent research and information retrieval skills *(revision Jan. '09)*

OPERATIONAL OBJECTIVE NO. 1: Continue with face-to-face information literacy instruction for both individuals and groups

	ACTION STEPS	DESIRABLE OUTCOMES	CRITERIA OF SUCCESS	EVALUATION STRATEGY	PRIMARY ACCOUNTABILITY	SCHEDULE Start – Completion	RESOURCES REQUIRED	STRATEGIC ALIGNMENT
1	Provide more collaborative learning areas and multimedia classrooms—*Lib. Mtg. Rooms equipped Summer'07.*	More effective collaboration for more students	Usage data shows growth	Usage data, user surveys	*ITS, Dir*, Information Literacy Comm.	2008–2011	Fujitsu Grant	Unparalleled 1-1
	Construct a larger library electronic classroom—*Plans developed Summer '07, reviewed by ITS.Sub to bud. Comm 09*	Larger classroom for hands-on construction	Expanded use of Information Literacy Services	Usage data	*ITS, Dir.*, Info. Lit. Comm.	2009, summer	$140K	Unparalleled 1-1

GOAL 1 : Information Literacy and Education—To develop activities promoting excellent research and information retrieval skills *(revision Jan. '09)*

OPERATIONAL OBJECTIVE NO. 2: Increase the amount of non face-to-face information literacy instruction to ensure that all members of the university community are reached.

	ACTION STEPS	DESIRABLE OUTCOMES	CRITERIA OF SUCCESS	EVALUATION STRATEGY	PRIMARY ACCOUNTABILITY	SCHEDULE Start – Completion	RESOURCES REQUIRED	STRATEGIC ALIGNMENT
1	Employ course-related Virtual Learning Services	CMS, Pod casting, blogging employed	Services are started and used	User feedback, surveys	Ref. Disc. Group	2006-09	Existing	Unparalleled 1-1, Innovative 2-3
2	Employ Library VRS—*Done Summer '07 for Fall '07*	Email, Chat, VRL—*IM Reference Fall'07*	Services are used and grow	User feedback, surveys	Ref. Staff	2006-2008	$0.00	Unparalleled 1-1
3	Develop more online tutorials	More tutorials on more topics	Web count	User feedback, surveys, focus groups	Ref. Staff	Ongoing	Existing budget	Unparalleled 1-1
4	Repository software for database of digital materials **CONTENTdm acquired '08**	Archive of electronic materials produced by faculty, students	Acquired and implemented	Count of items, use	Ref. & Archives staff	20012-20015	$4.5K '08, 4.5K'09	Unparalleled 1-1

GOAL 1 : Information Literacy and Education—To develop activities promoting excellent research and information retrieval skills *(revision Jan. '09)*

OPERATIONAL OBJECTIVE NO. 3: Increase the amount and enhance the quality of collaboration that goes on between teaching faculty and librarians.

	ACTION STEPS	DESIRABLE OUTCOMES	CRITERIA OF SUCCESS	EVALUATION STRATEGY	PRIMARY ACCOUNTABILITY	SCHEDULE Start – Completion	RESOURCES REQUIRED	STRATEGIC ALIGNMENT
1	Acquire campus-wide courseware management system.*Responsibility relocted to Provost's Office.*	Ability of librarians to provide services via CMS	CMS is acquired	Lbns. Assist users of CMS to incorporate library services	Head Ref., Head PS	2010		Unparalleled 1-1
2	Use campus LMS by integrating libns. Into classes	Provide ind. Inst. & consultl, integrate subj. guides.	Participation granted, students access services	Assessment tool of LMS	Ref/liaisons, Info Lit Comm	Upon consideration & acq of LMS	Univ capital	Unparalleled 1-1
3	Use LMS for lib tutorials and non-credit classes for Info Lit instruction & research	Greater access by students to libns for ind instruction	Participation	Stats assessment tool of LMS	Ref/liaisons, Info Lit Comm	2010- or post acq. Of LMS	Univ cap.	Unparalleled 1-1

GOAL 1 : Information Literacy and Education–To develop activities promoting excellent research and information retrieval skills *(revision Jan. '09)*

OPERATIONAL OBJECTIVE NO. 4: Incorporate assessment of information literacy skills throughout the college experience

	ACTION STEPS	DESIRABLE OUTCOMES	CRITERIA OF SUCCESS	EVALUATION STRATEGY	PRIMARY ACCOUNTABILITY	SCHEDULE Start – Completion	RESOURCES REQUIRED	STRATEGIC ALIGNMENT
1	Campus-wide CMS is acquired & used. *Restatement–Library uses CMS as appropriate.*	Acquisition of assessment data from system	CMS is acquired & assessment tools used	Use of CMS eval. Tools, User satisfaction surveys	Info. Lit. Comm.	2010+		Unparalleled 1-1
2	Conceive more professional reference office space for Ref. staff in conjunction with Commons concept	More professional and efficient area for personal productivity and student consult	Areas designed and constructed	Personal evaluation	Ref lbns	TBD	TBD	Employer 1st, Unparalleled 1-1

GOAL 2 : (Provide adequate resources for teaching and research. *(revision Jan. '09)*

OPERATIONAL OBJECTIVE NO.1: Increase the number of print and electronic resources acquired by the library to better support the curriculum

	ACTION STEPS	DESIRABLE OUTCOMES	CRITERIA OF SUCCESS	EVALUATION STRATEGY	PRIMARY ACCOUNTABILITY	SCHEDULE Start – Completion	RESOURCES REQUIRED	STRATEGIC ALIGNMENT
1	Acquire complete JSTOR offerings (completed July '06)	More research materials for students and faculty	Acquired	Examine JSTOR user data	Director, Head TS	2006 -	$50,505	Unparalleled 1-1
2	Increase book budget	More resources to support curriculum	Budget shows growth, materials on site	Budget analysis	Director, Head Acq., Head TS.	Postponed by Budget Reallocation	10% per year, book/$20K	Unparalleled 1-1
3	Increase serials budget	More resources to support curriculum	Budget shows growth, materials on site	Budget analysis	Head of Tech Servs. Head of Cat. & Serials	Postponed by Budget Reallocation	10% per year, $40K	Unparalleled 1-1
4	Acquire GLBT, CINAHL *(Completed FY '07)*	More resources to support curriculum	Budget shows growth, materials on site	User Stats	Dir., Head of Ref.	2007-2008	$14.5K	Unparalleled 1-1
5	Acquire Psychoanalytic Electronic Publications-- Postponed 09 budget constraints	More resources to support curriculum	Budget shows growth, materials on site	User Stats	Dir., Head of PS, Head TS	2012	$3.5K	Unparalleled 1-1
6	Acquire Psych. Books– postpponed 09 budget constraints	More resources to support curriculum	Budget shows growth, materials on site	User Stats	Dir., Head of PS, Head TS	2012	$3.6K	Unparalleled 1-1
7	Acq. Soc. Index w/full text	More resources to support curr	Budget allows additional purchase	User Stats	Dir., Head of PS, Head TS	Acauired 08	Existing	Unparalleled 1-1
8	Edu Index retrospective	More resources to support curr	Budget allows additional purchase	User stats	Dir. Head of PS, Head TS	Postponed	Postponed budget constraints	Unparallelled 1-1
9	Web of Science	More resources to support science education	Budget allows	User statae.	Diread, head PS, Head TS	Postponed	175,000 initial purchase	Unparallelled

GOAL 2 :Provide adequate resources for teaching and research   *(Jan. 09)*

OPERATIONAL OBJECTIVE NO. 2: Increase accessibility of electronic resources through additional physical access points and system functionality

	ACTION STEPS	DESIRABLE OUTCOMES	CRITERIA OF SUCCESS	EVALUATION STRATEGY	PRIMARY ACCOUNTABILITY	SCHEDULE Start – Completion	RESOURCES REQUIRED	STRATEGIC ALIGNMENT
1	Acquire enhanced technological capabilities	Greater tech. capability for use and management of resources	Resources acquired	User data	Head TS, MMCS, FTC	2006-2010	$120K on hold	Unparalleled 1-1
2	Enhance system functionality by acquiring serials load, Link resolver, federated search engine, ERM, Research & Discovery tool	Greater sophistication in system use	Acquired	User data, surveys	Head TS, PS	2006-2011 Requested for Fed Search/Link Resol. Submitted to budget comm 09	$68K + $27.5K per year *(Revised pricing being obtained Fall '07 A-Z serials link 08*	Unparalleled 1-1, Student Centered
3	Distance Education Capabilities	Supply distance students with more Widener resources	System in place	Usage data	Head PS	2006-2011	$2K/year	Unparalleled 1-1, Student Centered
4	Adaptive Tech.	Provide up-to-date adaptive technology to use information resources	Systems upgraded	With ENABLE, assess need, use	Head MMCS	2006-2011	TBD	Unparalleled 1-1, Student Centered
5	Archival Digitation	Selected resources digitized and preserved–acq & use of ContentDM	Successful digitation of collectins provided	Monitor time, cost, perceived value	Archivist	2007-	$9.8K initial, 3.2K/year. Begun AY 08	Unparalleled, Innovative
6	Hire Full-Time Archivst no new positions 08, 09	New Staff Members Archives	Hired	Archives Stats, Personnel Evaluation	Archivist	Postponed - Bud. Reall.	$66,600	Unparalleled, Innovative

O
AL Goal 3: Facilities to provide a high-quality research, study and work environment.

OPERATIONAL OBJECTIVE NO. 1: Acquire new archival storage area.

	ACTION STEPS	DESIRABLE OUTCOMES	CRITERIA OF SUCCESS	EVALUATION STRATEGY	PRIMARY ACCOUNTABILITY	SCHEDULE Start – Completion	RESOURCES REQUIRED	STRATEGIC ALIGNMENT
1	Acquire language lab space, shelving, additional space	A unified storage space for current resources and future donations	Space is acquired		Director, Archivist	2010 began…estimates for compact shelving asked for '09	Cap. Approx $75K	Unparalleled 1-1

O
AL Goal 3: Facilities to provide a high-quality research, study and work environment.

OPERATIONAL OBJECTIVE NO. 2: Reference – Provide a collaborative learning on the main level.

	ACTION STEPS	DESIRABLE OUTCOMES	CRITERIA OF SUCCESS	EVALUATION STRATEGY	PRIMARY ACCOUNTABILITY	SCHEDULE Start – Completion	RESOURCES REQUIRED	STRATEGIC ALIGNMENT
1	Provide space for collaborative learning–to be assessed in conjunction with "Commons" ideas	Area in Reference where students can work collaboratively using a wide variety of information technology	Students use the resources	User statistics	Director, Head of Reference, *ITS*	2010–	$10,500 to provide kiosk and equipment, furniture, scanners	Unparalleled 1-1, Innovative 1-1

O
AL Goal 3: Facilities to provide a high-quality research, study and work environment.

OPERATIONAL OBJECTIVE NO. 4: Renovate Reference Area

	ACTION STEPS	DESIRABLE OUTCOMES	CRITERIA OF SUCCESS	EVALUATION STRATEGY	PRIMARY ACCOUNTABILITY	SCHEDULE Start – Completion	RESOURCES REQUIRED	STRATEGIC ALIGNMENT
1	Redesign Reference and Public Services areas to provide lobby with single point of service incl. cleaning/painting of Ref. area	Control access to facility, provide a unified service point, add larger electronic classroom	Elements are acquired	Usage statistics	Director, Heads of Reference and Public Services, plus operations	2010–	$300k- $400K	Unparalleled 1-1

O
A Goal 3: Facilities to provide a high-quality research, study and work environment.

OPERATIONAL OBJECTIVE NO. 5: Multimedia and Classroom Support

	ACTION STEPS	DESIRABLE OUTCOMES	CRITERIA OF SUCCESS	EVALUATION STRATEGY	PRIMARY ACCOUNTABILITY	SCHEDULE Start – Completion	RESOURCES REQUIRED	STRATEGIC ALIGNMENT
1	Redesign 106 as an information commons and the Electronic Classroom as a viewing room—*Will require re-visioning as result of ITS reorganization.*	Provide students with ability to use and view electronic materials	Installation of facility	Usage statistics	Director, Lib. Faculty, ITS	TBD after Electronic Classroom is relocated and 106 is not needed for classes 106 relocated 08	$65k - 106, $20K viewing area or $250K from outside resources depending upon plan	Unparalleled, Student Centered

O
AL Goal 3: Facilities to provide a high-quality research, study and work environment.

OPERATIONAL OBJECTIVE NO. 6: General

	ACTION STEPS	DESIRABLE OUTCOMES	CRITERIA OF SUCCESS	EVALUATION STRATEGY	PRIMARY ACCOUNTABILITY	SCHEDULE Start – Completion	RESOURCES REQUIRED	STRATEGIC ALIGNMENT
1	Replace HVAC *(Completed Spring '07)*	Better climate control for work area and study	Work Completed in May	Daily temperature assessment	Head of Operations.	2006	$400K	Unparalleled, Student Centered, Employer of 1st Choice
2	ADA Compliance Audit	Push Buttons and Lower Level Power Automatic Doors on Library Lower Level	Audit Report Rec'd.	Installation	Director	2009	$4K	Student Centered, Employee 1st Choice
3	Fire Code Audit	Confidence in Evacuation Efficiency	Audit Report Rec'd.	Report from Fire Marshall	Director	2010	Existing Budget	Student Centered, Employee 1st Choice
4	Recarpet Library	Increased perception of library as clean and pleasant environment	Carpet installed	Visual inspection	Dir. President	2011	Capital, $194,500	Student Cent., Employer
5	Assess cleaning/painting of concrete, walls	Cleaner, lighter, more comfortable facility for use	Assessment made proposals accepted funded	User stats, surveys	Dir, President, President's architectural consults.	2009	TBD	Student Cent., Employer, Unparallelled
6	Plan for newer furniture	Cleaner, more pleasant comfortable facility	Assessments made and proposals funded	User state, surveys	Dir, President, President's architectual consults.	2010	TBD	Stu. Cent, Employer, Unparallelled

O
AL Goal 4: Safety and security – create a well-maintained and staffed library space that provides the safety and security of the Library's users, personnel and resources.

OPERATIONAL OBJECTIVE NO. 1: Install a one-card entry/exit system for the Library

	ACTION STEPS	DESIRABLE OUTCOMES	CRITERIA OF SUCCESS	EVALUATION STRATEGY	PRIMARY ACCOUNTABILITY	SCHEDULE Start – Completion	RESOURCES REQUIRED	STRATEGIC ALIGNMENT
1	Acquire and install system and turnstiles & reconfigure entrance for enhanced safety and security.	Enhanced protection for library staff user resources, better monitoring of facilities	Installation and use	Stats, changes in incident reports	Director, Head of Public Services, Plus Operations	Fall 2009	$125K	Student Centered, Employer
2	*Alternative to Goal 4, OO1— develop and present plan for security with p/t campus safety officers on duty to examine IDs and allow only authorized persons at all times library is open. Draft in hands of Head of Campus Safety Summer '07*	Enha nced protection for staff, users, resources	Campus safety acquires staffing and plan is executed	Observation, comparison of incident reports, user/visitor feedback	Director, Head of PS, Head of Campus Safety, University Executive Team re: policies.	Fall 2008	Approx $100K staffing	Student-centered, Employer of first choice.

O
AL Goal 4: Safety and security – create a well-maintained and staffed library space that provides the safety and security of the Library's users, personnel and resources.

OPERATIONAL OBJECTIVE NO. 2: Install duress alarm

	ACTION STEPS	DESIRABLE OUTCOMES	CRITERIA OF SUCCESS	EVALUATION STRATEGY	PRIMARY ACCOUNTABILITY	SCHEDULE Start -- Completion	RESOURCES REQUIRED	STRATEGIC ALIGNMENT
1	Install more phones/alarms - *Additional phone added at Reference desk–Spring '07*	Increased sense of security & actual increase in security	Installation	Use	Directory, Campus Safety, Operations	2007 -	TBD	Student Centered, Employer of First Choice

O
AL Goal 4: Safety and security – create a well-maintained and staffed library space that provides the safety and security of the Library's users, personnel and resources.

OPERATIONAL OBJECTIVE NO. 3: Crate Library Taskforce to review safety/awareness

	ACTION STEPS	DESIRABLE OUTCOMES	CRITERIA OF SUCCESS	EVALUATION STRATEGY	PRIMARY ACCOUNTABILITY	SCHEDULE Start -- Completion	RESOURCES REQUIRED	STRATEGIC ALIGNMENT
1	Create Taskforce & develop security plan	Increased worker awareness of security, policies, procedures	Taskforce created, information shared	Minutes of meetings	Director & Exec.	2009-	Current staff & Budget	Employer, Students
2	Taskforce–monitors, signage, way finding, lighting, cleanliness, evaluate entry steps for safety improvements, enhance housekeeping and security.	More efficient use patterns	Cleaner facility	Periodic Inspection	Taskforce, Director, Building Coordinator, Operations, Campus Safety	Fall 2009	Current Budget and Staff	Employee of 1st Choice, Student Centered

O
AL Goal 5: Instructional technology – Assign current and emerging instructional technologies to enhance classroom environment.

OPERATIONAL OBJECTIVE NO. 1: Manage Multimedia Classroom

	ACTION STEPS	DESIRABLE OUTCOMES	CRITERIA OF SUCCESS	EVALUATION STRATEGY	PRIMARY ACCOUNTABILITY	SCHEDULE Start -- Completion	RESOURCES REQUIRED	STRATEGIC ALIGNMENT
1	Install more sophisticated management system in multimedia classroom– *Responsibility shifted to ITS Fall '07*	More efficient use of resources, speedier service response	Fewer deliveries because of outages	Department Staff	ITS	2007- 2011	TBD – will depend upon systems and comprehensiveness	Unparalleled 1-1
2	Create Information Commons	Spaces for individual and group, media production viewing	Students able to do hands-on media	Department Staff, Teaching Faculty	Department Staff, Teaching Faculty	2008	TBD	Unparalleled, Student Centered
3	Increase Number of Multimedia Rooms to 100%– *Responsibility shifted to ITS Fall '07*	More efficient use of resources, speedier service response	Fewer deliveries because of outages	Department Staff	ITS	2007-2020	$40K/per year @ 2 rooms per year	Unparalleled

O
AL Goal 5: Instructional technology – Assign current and emerging instructional technologies to enhance classroom environment.

OPERATIONAL OBJECTIVE NO. 2: Develop asset management schedule for equipping multimedia classroom

	ACTION STEPS	DESIRABLE OUTCOMES	CRITERIA OF SUCCESS	EVALUATION STRATEGY	PRIMARY ACCOUNTABILITY	SCHEDULE Start -- Completion	RESOURCES REQUIRED	STRATEGIC ALIGNMENT
1	Acquire funds to replace aging equipment– *Responsibility shifted to ITS Fall '07*	Reasonable replacement of equipment with available	Fewer equipment failures	Statistics of use	Head of Multimedia and Classroom Support	2008 -	28,000/year	Unparalleled

O
AL Goal 5: Instructional technology – Assign current and emerging instructional technologies to enhance classroom environment.

OPERATIONAL OBJECTIVE NO. 3: Implement a single CMS/LMS online

	ACTION STEPS	DESIRABLE OUTCOMES	CRITERIA OF SUCCESS	EVALUATION STRATEGY	PRIMARY ACCOUNTABILITY	SCHEDULE Start -- Completion	RESOURCES REQUIRED	STRATEGIC ALIGNMENT
1	Acquire single full-featured industry-standard LMS for campus–Responsibility shifted to Provost Summer '07	Support for modern LMS *Responsibility to Provost Office*	Installation, usage	Usage statistics, focus groups	Head of Faculty Technology Center	2010	$300K	Unparalleled

O
AL

OPERATIONAL OBJECTIVE NO. 4: Conduct a study of peer Institution Teaching and Learning Curve

	ACTION STEPS	DESIRABLE OUTCOMES	CRITERIA OF SUCCESS	EVALUATION STRATEGY	PRIMARY ACCOUNTABILITY	SCHEDULE Start – Completion	RESOURCES REQUIRED	STRATEGIC ALIGNMENT
1	Survey peer institutions– *Responsibility shifted to Provost's Office Sumer '07*	Develop a model of a TLC for Widener	Design/model is obtained	Usage statistics, user satisfaction	Director, Head of Faculty Technology Center	2005-2006	Current Budget	Innovative - (1-3)

O
AL Goal 5: Instructional technology – Assign current and emerging instructional technologies to enhance classroom environment. *Responsibility shifted to Provost Summer '07*

OPERATIONAL OBJECTIVE NO. 5: Conduct a study of peer Institution Teaching and Learning Centers

	ACTION STEPS	DESIRABLE OUTCOMES	CRITERIA OF SUCCESS	EVALUATION STRATEGY	PRIMARY ACCOUNTABILITY	SCHEDULE Start – Completion	RESOURCES REQUIRED	STRATEGIC ALIGNMENT
1	Develop inventory Hardware/Software/Expertise for Web-based instruction-To Provost '07	Ascertain Faculty Income		Interview Faculty	Head of FTC	2007-2010	Graduate Assistant, Grants	Unparalleled
2	Increase Technical Resources–*Responsibility to Provost Office '07*	Additional Space, Better Equipment, More Work Stations	Development of Space/Equipment Acquired	User Stats, Faculty Focus Groups	Head of FTC	2009-2015	Grants	Unparalleled

O
AL Goal 6: Insure that the appropriate amount, type and level of information resources are acquired and maintained for instruction and research on campus.

OPERATIONAL OBJECTIVE NO. 1: Analyze the collection

	ACTION STEPS	DESIRABLE OUTCOMES	CRITERIA OF SUCCESS	EVALUATION STRATEGY	PRIMARY ACCOUNTABILITY	SCHEDULE Start – Completion	RESOURCES REQUIRED	STRATEGIC ALIGNMENT
1	Acquire WorldCat Collection Analysis Service	A collection of information that meets current and future needs of Widener students and faculty	Project begins, statistics analyzed	Continual evaluation of collection and purchases	Head of Acquisitions, Collection Development Committee	2010	$3,000	Unparalleled 1-1

O
AL Goal 7: Metropolitan Region

OPERATIONAL OBJECTIVE NO. 1: Assist and support the University's efforts to enhance the metro region.

	ACTION STEPS	DESIRABLE OUTCOMES	CRITERIA OF SUCCESS	EVALUATION STRATEGY	PRIMARY ACCOUNTABILITY	SCHEDULE Start – Completion	RESOURCES REQUIRED	STRATEGIC ALIGNMENT
1	Support Programs on All Non-Chester Campuses	Effective Program in the Region	Continuing and Successful Programs	Enrollment, Revenues	Dir., Head of PS, M&CS, FTC	2007 -	Adequate Personnel and Equipment for Campus	Metro
2	Participate Effectively in Regional Consortia	Contributor/Participant in Information Sharing	Statistics Showing Sharing and Visitation	Stats	Dir., LibFac, Staff	2007 -	Membership Fees, Current Library Budget	Metro
3	Provide Library Access to Local High School Students	Better Research Skills in Local Schools	Continued Use by Local Students	Stats of Use, Entrance Use	Head PS, Ref	2007 -	Current Staff and Budget	Metro
4	Provide Access and Internet Use to Local Community Members–**Will be reassessed '09**	A More Informed Public	Observed Use of Non-Game Sites	Sign-up Stats, Observation	Head Ref., Dir.	2007 -	Current Staff & Budget	Metro
5	Providing Service to Widener Partnership Charter School as requested	More Educated Elem. Students in Area	National and State Test Scores	National and State Tests	Dir.	2007 -	Current Staff and Budget Grants	Metro
6	Planning for Access PA for Non-Widener Use	More Appropriate Resources to Support Growing "Public Library" Activities	Stats of Use	Stats	Dir., Head TS	2007 -	Current Staff and Budget	Metro

o

AL Goal 8: Employer of First Choice

OPERATIONAL OBJECTIVE NO. 1: Make Wolfgram a more desirable place to work.

	ACTION STEPS	DESIRABLE OUTCOMES	CRITERIA OF SUCCESS	EVALUATION STRATEGY	PRIMARY ACCOUNTABILITY	SCHEDULE Start – Completion	RESOURCES REQUIRED	STRATEGIC ALIGNMENT
1	Maintain Accessible Entrance–**Upgrade requested in 10 capital**	Free Access to Disabled	Greater use by Disabled Students, Community and Staff	Observation	Dir., Operations	2007 -	TBD, Elevator Renovations, Door $4K	Employee of First Choice
2	Supporting Employee Training via Consortia	A More Aware Workforce	Constantly Evolving Skill Sets for Staff	Annual Reviews	Dir., Supervisors	2007 -	Current Budget	Employee of First Choice
3	Continual Review of Safety in Building - **See Goal 4, OO3**	Safe Workplace	Fewer Incidents	Incident Reports	Dir., B.C., Campus Safety Operations	2007 -	Existing Budget	Employee of First Choice
4	Planning Facility Upgrades For Comfort, Cleanliness	Cleaner, Healthier Building	Fewer Complaints	Observation, Periodic Review	Dir., Staff, Operations	2007 -	Existing Budget, Strategic Initiative, Capital	Employee of First Choice
5	Support Staff Continuing and Personal Education	Well-rounded, well-educated Staff	Courses Taken, Degrees Awarded	Maintain Reports, Annual Evaluation	Dir., Supervisors	2007 -	Flexible Schedules	Employee of First Choice

o

AL Goal 9: Student Centeredness

OPERATIONAL OBJECTIVE NO. 1: Providing expanded services to students.

	ACTION STEPS	DESIRABLE OUTCOMES	CRITERIA OF SUCCESS	EVALUATION STRATEGY	PRIMARY ACCOUNTABILITY	SCHEDULE Start – Completion	RESOURCES REQUIRED	STRATEGIC ALIGNMENT
1	Maintain Accessibility – *Accessible door maintained via monitoring, service calls, appropriate signage.*	Accessibility	Easier Accessibility	Observation	Dir., Head of PS, Build. Coord., Operation	2007 -	Existing Budget Capital	Student Centered
2	Knowing and Responding to Student Safety Concerns	Greater Safety	Fewer Complaints	Incident Reports	Dir., Head of PS, BC. Campus Safety	2007 -	Existing Budget Capital	Student Centered
3	Keeping Library Open 24 Hours During Exams– *Program modified Fall 08 by budget*	More Study Spaces	Faculty and Student Feedback	Stats	Dir., Campus Safety	2008 -	Existing Budget, Campus Safety Officers	Student Centered
4	Recognizing Student Workers with Pizza Party– **Disallowed by Finance Dept.**	Happier Student Workers	Students Return to Work	Retention Studies	Dir., Circ. Supervisor	2007 -	Existing Budget	Student Centered
5	Relocate and Expand Library Electronic Classroom–**See Goal 1**	Better Teaching/Learning Area	Built/Used	Student Assessment, Faculty Feedback	Dir.	2009 -	$130K	Student Centered
6	Acquire III Module for Single Search Across Databases– *To be reassessed upon arrival of Law's Associate Dean for Information Services and Director of the Law Library. See g2 002, AS2*	Easier to Use Library System	Acquired/Use	System Stats., Student Focus Groups	Dir., Ref. Librarians, Head of TS	2008 -		Student Centered

O								
AL	Goal 10: Diversity							

OPERATIONAL OBJECTIVE NO. 1: Participate in University's diversity efforts.

	ACTION STEPS	DESIRABLE OUTCOMES	CRITERIA OF SUCCESS	EVALUATION STRATEGY	PRIMARY ACCOUNTABILITY	SCHEDULE Start -- Completion	RESOURCES REQUIRED	STRATEGIC ALIGNMENT
1	Celebrate World Cultures via Displays of Books and Artifacts—*Display of Docs & artifacts re: Immigration, Civil Rights, major world religious celebrations, multiculturalism and ethnicity.*	Continual Awareness of Others	Displays Continue	Observation	Dir., Ref. Librarians	2006 -	Existing Budget	Diversity
2	Book Club Topics Show Wide Range of Cultures, Lifestyles	Awareness of Cultures	Discussions	Observation, Focus Groups	Dir., Head of PS, Ref. Librarians	2005 -	Existing Budget	Diversity
3	Welcoming a Diverse Workforce	Mixture of Peoples	Observable Diversity	Stats	Dir., HR	2005 -	Existing Budget	Diversity
4	Welcoming a Diverse Student Workforce	Mixture of Peoples	Observable Diversity	Stats	Dir.	2007 -	Additional Money to Hire Non-Work Study, $12/year	Diversity

Schmidt Library Long Range Plan

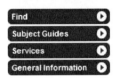

Find ⊙
Subject Guides ⊙
Services ⊙
General Information ⊙

THE COLLEGE OF 2020: STUDENTS One of a series of reports on the future of higher education issued by The Chronicle of Higher Education Research Services. (The College of 2020 Executive Summary Report)

Long Range Plan 2007-2012
~ Vision Statement
~ Research and Teaching
~ Technology
~ Collections
~ Facilities
~ Communications/Community
~ Staff

Quick Links

IFL 101
Schmidt Library Catalog
Our Journal List
Research Help
Citation Help
FAQs

Hours
Staff
General Information - Map
Search Library Web Pages

More Quick Links ▾

Vision Statement

The faculty and staff of Schmidt Library are committed to providing high quality classroom and individualized instruction in research skills, state-of-the-art technology for information access, strong collections in support of the curriculum, and excellent space for research and study.

Research and Teaching

- Ensure that all YCP students are information literate to complete their YCP coursework and to meet success in their chosen careers
  - Continue pedagogical development of IFL101, addressing Middle States Report

    Timeline: Annual and ongoing

    Leaders: Instruction Librarian, Library Faculty

    Assessment: Student surveys, grade distribution, faculty feedback
  - Evaluate and revise syllabus, outcomes and eText on annual basis

    Timeline: Annual and ongoing

    Leaders: Instruction Librarian, all Library Faculty

    Assessment: Student surveys, grade distribution, annual retreat outcomes

- Foster collaboration with all faculty for integration of cohesive core curriculum literacies

  o Work closely with faculty in Writing, Human Communications and Mathematics to provide incoming freshmen a common learning experience that reinforces concepts learned in each discipline

    Timeline: Annual and ongoing

    Leaders: Library Director, Instruction Librarian, Chairs, Program Coordinators, Dean of Academic Affairs, and Academic Senate Academic Programs Committee

    Assessment: To be determined

  o Encourage development of systematic assessment of the core

    Timeline: Establish a schedule for periodic review

    Leaders: Library Director, Instruction Librarian, Chairs, Program Coordinators, Dean of Academic Affairs, and Academic Programs Committee

    Assessment: To be determined

- Facilitate implementation of course management software, teaching tools and electronic resources to provide excellent support for teaching and learning

  o Provide training for all faculty to develop skills in the integration of teaching, learning, and technology, including course management software.

    Timeline: Began 2006 and ongoing

    Leaders: Instructional Media Librarian, Instruction Librarian,

    Instructional Resources Committee

    Assessment: To be determined

  o Provide information and demonstrations of relevant technology. Interview all new faculty each year to discuss instructional media needs.

    Timeline: Began 2005 and ongoing

    Leaders: Instructional Media Librarian, Instructional Resources Committee

    Assessment: Interviews, surveys, workshop evaluations

  o Offer faculty workshops every semester for training in software and equipment for classroom instruction

    Timeline: Began 2006 and ongoing

    Leaders: Instruction Librarian, Instructional Media Librarian

    Assessment: Interviews, surveys, workshop evaluations

- Provide advanced instruction and research assistance to all college communities

  - Investigate and recommend a web tutorial solution

    Timeline: Begin Fall 2007

    Leaders: Instruction Librarian, Systems Librarian, Instructional Media Librarian

    Assessment: To be determined

  - Explore options for virtual research services, help for remote users, and online tutorials

    Timeline: Began Fall 2006

    Leaders: Instruction Librarian, Systems Librarian

    Assessment: To be determined

Technology

- Work with Information Technology to create and support a comprehensive virtual library environment, integrated with all campus systems

  - Continue regular Information Technology and Library management team meetings

    Timeline: Ongoing

    Leaders: All Library Faculty

    Assessment: To be determined

- Sustain dynamic environment with state-of-the-art technology, wireless and wired capacity, with commensurate bandwidth and hardware

  - Promote laptop, notebook, and handheld devices for faculty and students
  - Investigate ways to provide streaming media services across campus

    Timeline: Ongoing, long-term (possible capital implications)

    Leaders: Instructional Media Librarian, Collection Development Librarian, Systems Librarian, Information Technology

    Assessment: To be determined

  - Create Instructional Media Lab for faculty (possible capital implications)

    Timeline: 2010

    Leaders: Instructional Media Librarian, Systems Librarian, Information Technology, Instructional Resources Committee

    Assessment: To be determined

- Enhance Schmidt Library web site and investigate portal services, integrating them with college's website

  - Redesign web site

    Timeline: Summer 2007

Leaders: Systems Librarian and Information Technology

Assessment: Ongoing assessment survey

o Investigate SirsiDynix portal solution

Timeline: SirsiDynix timetable

Leader: Systems Librarian

Assessment: To be determined

- Provide state-of-the-art instructional media to all classrooms

    o Work with Information Technology to provide additional smart classrooms across campus

    Timeline: Ongoing

    Leaders: Instructional Media Librarian, Information Technology, Instructional Resources Committee

    Assessment: Instructional Media survey, Instructional Resources Committee feedback

    o Define and develop Instructional Media role to support West Campus services including equipment, manpower and logistical support

    Timeline: Ongoing

    Leaders: Instructional Media Librarian, Information Technology, Dean of Academic Affairs, Dean of Campus Operations, Instructional Resources Committee

    Assessment: Faculty survey

    o Communicate with faculty and administration for all current and future renovation issues regarding instructional media. Prepare a plan for budget, resources and services for new buildings.

    Timeline: Ongoing

    Leaders: Instructional Media Librarian, Information Services Librarians, Information Technology, Instructional Resources Committee

    Assessment: To be determined

- Integrate and clarify online systems and delivery of services

    o Monitor commercial vendor products developing web search tools to link services for users

    Timeline: Ongoing

    Leaders: Systems Librarian, Collection Development Librarian

    Assessment: Annual survey

    o Investigate usability testing

    Timeline: 2008

    Leaders: Systems Librarian

    Assessment: Hands-on testing

Collections

Provide information resources of all types in support of all curricula

- o Work with faculty to develop collections

  Timeline: Ongoing

  Leaders: Collection Development Librarian, Library Faculty

  Assessment: Annual survey

- o Advocate budget support for ongoing information resources such as subscription databases

  Timeline: Ongoing

  Leaders: Library Director, Collection Development Librarian

  Assessment: Annual survey

- o Continue to add media and investigate emerging multimedia formats and their delivery to faculty and students

  Timeline: Ongoing

  Leaders: Collection Development Librarian, Instructional Media Librarian, Systems Librarian

  Assessment: Annual survey

- Assure preservation, protection, digitization, and access for all library collections

  - o Implement ContentDM

    Timeline: Ongoing

    Leaders: Systems Librarian, Information Services Librarians

    Assessment: Public access and use statistics

- Use collection development and analysis tools systematically to build collections

  - o Implement SirsiDynix Directors Station

    Timeline: 2007

    Leaders: Systems Librarian, Collection Development Librarian

    Assessment: To be determined

  - o Implement Serials Solutions Electronic Resource Management system to streamline ordering, technical support, and digital rights management

    Timeline: Ongoing

    Leaders: Collection Development Librarian, Systems Librarian

    Assessment: To be determined

- Investigate Serials Solutions statistics management solution

    Timeline: When available from vendor

    Leaders: Systems Librarian, Collection Development Librarian

    Assessment: Consolidated statistics, reduction of staff time

- Maintain strong consortial relationships to expand YCP access to information resources

    Timeline: Ongoing

    Leaders: Library Director, Library Faculty

    Assessment: Annual survey

- Develop collection policies

  - Develop collection development policies for major subject areas

    Timeline: 2008-09

    Leaders: Collection Development Librarian, Library Faculty

    Assessment: To be determined

  - Formalize a collection development policy for Archives and Special Collections

    Timeline: 2008-09

    Leaders: Collection Development Librarian, Information Services Librarians

    Assessment: Annual survey

Facilities

- Provide atmosphere conducive to active learning through well-designed user, staff, and collection spaces

  - Expand network, electrical, and wireless infrastructures to support more workstations, laptops, and other portable information devices

    Timeline: Ongoing

    Leaders: Library Director, Systems Librarian, Information Services Librarians, Information Technology, Dean of Campus Operations

    Assessment: Annual survey

  - Evaluate library collection, user space, and staff space and reallocate space to support changing demands

    Timeline: Ongoing

    Leaders: Library Director, Information Services Librarians

    Assessment: Annual surveys

  - Explore option to offer IFL classrooms as open computer labs during late nights and weekends

    Timeline: Ongoing

    Leaders: Instruction Librarian, Information Services Librarians, Systems Librarian, Information Technology

    Assessment: To be determined

      o Examine practices and policies for scheduling hours

           Timeline: 2006

           Leaders: Information Services Librarians

           Assessment: Annual survey

- Collaborate with the YCP administration, consortia, and local authorities to develop a comprehensive disaster preparedness plan for continuity and recovery

           Timeline: 2010

           Leaders: Library Faculty

           Assessment: To be determined

Communications/Community

- Develop and implement communications strategies to inform all YCP communities of new and existing services, collections, search tools, etc.
- Build community by co-sponsoring lectures, seminars, exhibits, and other programs with other YCP departments and York city and county organizations

           Timeline: Ongoing

           Leaders: Library Director, Library Faculty

           Assessment: Annual surveys

Staff

- Recruit necessary personnel whose knowledge and skills facilitate the library's mission
- Develop an organized system of ongoing staff training
- Foster staff development
- Formalize student internship program

           Timeline: Ongoing

           Leaders: Library Faculty

           Assessment: Annual surveys

Resources

- http://www.pewinternet.org/ reports

- Perceptions of Libraries and Information Resources. OCLC report. 2005

- http://www.outsellinc.com/ reports

- Mission statements for college libraries. Association of College and Research Libraries. 1999.

- LISTSERVS

Mission Statement

Bowdoin College Library staff, services, resources, and collections advance the pursuit of knowledge and offer a gateway to the world of information and ideas. In support of that mission, the Library serves as an intellectual and cultural gathering place that fosters and enhances learning, education, research, and personal fulfillment.

Core Values

We believe:

- in the individual right to intellectual pursuit, free from censorship or violation of privacy;

- in nurturing the intellectual curiosity that leads to lifelong learning;

- in preserving connections to the past while embracing the challenges of the future;

- that in an ever-changing world, success depends upon flexibility, innovation and a constant reassessment of the needs of our community;

- that the strength of our library depends not only on its collections and services, but also on the quality of its staff;

- that the workplace should foster accomplishment, individual achievement and growth;

- in treating our colleagues and patrons with dignity, honesty, good humor, and a respect for social and cultural diversity; and

- that outstanding library service requires continuous collaboration, cooperation and clear communication.

The Bowdoin College Library Statement of Goals

Goal # 1: Develop collections and provide optimal access to information resources in support of academic programs of the College.

Goal #2: Offer library services and resources that sustain the curriculum and facilitate the research endeavors of faculty and students.

Goal #3: Promote the use of information technologies and serve as a teaching laboratory where new resources and services are introduced, explored and developed.

Goal #4: Enhance the educational experience of students at Bowdoin through teaching and promoting information literacy skills that are necessary to find, evaluate, and use information effectively.

Goal #5: Engage in a partnership with faculty in the educational process.

Goal #6: Promote the preservation and use of historical collections and archival records that serve the Bowdoin curriculum, College administrative programs, and the scholarly community.

Goal #7: Contribute to the intellectual, cultural, and recreational pursuits of the College beyond the classroom.

Goal #8: Build and continually develop a skilled staff equipped to meet the constantly changing needs of the Library and the campus community.

Goal # 9: Create a well-equipped and technologically up-to-date library facility providing both users and staff with an attractive, comfortable, safe environment conducive to work, study, and learning.

Goal #10: Enhance access to information resources and services through coordinated participation in regional, national, and international programs and initiatives.

Goal #11: Promote the library profession and represent its ethics and standards through leadership on campus, in the profession, and within the community at large.

Goal # 12: Offer information resources to individuals outside the campus community, in coordination with other libraries and cultural organizations.

The Bowdoin College Library Strategic Plan for 2008 – 2010:

Objective I.	**Build Library Collections**
Strategy A.	Collection development and access
Strategy B.	Collection maintenance
Strategy C.	Archiving, records management, and preservation
Strategy D.	Scholarly communication and digital asset management
Strategy E.	Digital content development
Objective II.	**Enhance Instruction, Research Support, and Public Programming**
Strategy A.	Instruction
Strategy B.	Research support
Strategy C.	Point-of-need access to resources
Strategy D.	Point-of-need access to assistance
Strategy E.	Communication
Strategy F.	Public programming
Objective III.	**Strengthen Facilities and Infrastructure**
Strategy A.	Library space planning
Strategy B.	Technology infrastructure and equipment
Strategy C.	Security and preservation
Objective IV.	**Management, Training and Assessment**
Strategy A.	Management through teams and alliances
Strategy B.	Staff development and training
Strategy C.	Enterprise system software upgrades and implementation
Strategy D.	Statistics and assessment
Strategy E.	External funding and development
Objective V.	**Meet Professional Responsibilities**
Strategy A.	First Amendment issues and copyright policies
Strategy B.	Rights to privacy and confidentiality
Strategy C.	Recruitment for the profession

Objective I. Build Library Collections

To build a balanced library collection that effectively supports the Bowdoin curriculum and faculty research, librarians and faculty members must select the best information resources from the print and digital publishing worlds. Library staff adopt collaborative models and new and proven technologies to acquire, manage, preserve, provide access to, and ensure interconnectivity among resources in all formats. With these activities comes the responsibility to educate the community about new methods and strategies to publish, manage, and preserve electronic information for scholarly and administrative use.

Strategy A. Collection development and access
Select and make available balanced collections, in coordination with Colby and Bates Colleges. Provide seamless, ubiquitous access to information resources.

- Build faculty understanding of and support for collaborative efforts to develop a single CBB collection through continued outreach to faculty.
- Strengthen the role of librarians in discipline-related collection development and maintenance for all formats; review the role that faculty play in collection building within the context of a new collection liaison/CBB joint collection plan.
- Provide digital tools for faculty/librarian collection collaboration, and develop new procedures to ensure timely ordering and reduce emergency ordering.
- Develop collections to support the research and curricular needs of new faculty positions added through the capital campaign and of new programs, such as the Coastal Studies and Common Good Centers.
- Evaluate the existing catalog and enhancements within the context of the CBB next-generation catalog initiative.
- Examine the role of e-books in collection development; investigate new reader technology and options to incorporate e-book metadata and content, e.g., from Google Book Search and participating institutions.
- Enhance or update bibliographic records to broaden access to correlating digitized content.
- Improve Bowdoin WorldCat holdings by loading cataloging for unique archival and manuscript collections, U.S. government documents, digital serials and e-books.
- Establish project timetable to complete the retrospective conversion of remaining card catalog records for rare books to MARC21 electronic records, and initiate the project work plan.
- Pursue outsourcing opportunities for cataloging gift book collections, music materials, and authority control.

Strategy B. Collection maintenance
Ensure that library collections are well maintained and remain accessible to researchers over time. Develop policies based on national standards for format migration of print, analog media, and digital resources.

- Develop criteria and retention policies for print collections also held in trusted digital archives.

- Review criteria and plan for choosing materials to be stored off-site in the context of broader collection policies.
- Adopt collection strategies that incorporate best practices for format longevity.

Strategy C. Archiving, records management, and preservation

Assess the condition of materials in all formats known to be at risk; devise systematic preservation strategies for historic print collections, newsprint, audio-visual recordings, and in collaboration with IT, electronic records, including Web sites. Ensure that fulfillment of the College Archives mandate to preserve records of enduring value extends to digital records.

- Carry out a preservation assessment of the general Library collection in consultation with specialists; based on this assessment, develop short and long term action plans to incorporate basic preservation measures into current collection management policies and procedures.
- Undertake a preservation assessment survey of magnetic media and initiate procedures to refresh or migrate fragile recordings in Special Collections to digital formats.
- Enhance records management Web portal to provide a more usable interface for College administrative staff.
- Review existing records management schedules for College records to insure consideration of records in electronic format.

Strategy D. Scholarly communication and digital asset management

Inform faculty, students and staff about new publishing models and open access initiatives to create free, permanent, timely online dissemination of scholarship and research results. Devise campus-wide policies and strategies to address challenges of digital asset management.

- Initiate a campus-wide discussion of the merits of building an institutional repository of campus scholarship.
- Participate in campus-wide investigation, policy development, planning, and implementation of an institutional repository for digital objects in support of new modes of scholarly communication and the preservation, storage, and retrieval of institutional records.
- Explore issues related to digital access to honors projects.

- Continue discussions with faculty of new modes of scholarly communication and new models for supporting and promoting scholarly publishing; assist faculty efforts to adopt alternative publishing options.
- Foster campus discussions of new digital publishing technologies and related issues such as author fees, author rights, and scholarly communication trends.
- In collaboration with IT, plan the educational launch and promotion of new Digital Asset Management (DAM) guidelines for the management of digital images, video, and audio, including file standards, metadata, and workflow.

Strategy E. Digital content development

Digitize materials of enduring administrative value and scholarly interest, in collaboration with other College departments as well as with state and regional repositories that share collections of common interest.

- Explore digital publishing technologies (e.g., bepress) for all formats including print, audio, and visual materials.
- Develop process and configure systems to create EAD XML finding aids, and participate in test bed activities to develop cross-searching of manuscript collections within the State of Maine.
- Create a digital version of the James Bowdoin (III) Letterbooks.

Objective II. Enhance Instruction, Research Support and Public Programming

Students, faculty, and other library users seek support and assistance in navigating an expanding and increasingly complicated universe of information resources. At the same time, users have high expectations for self-reliance and personal control. Library staff help users form research strategies, find specific information, and acquire particular works through the use of electronic tools designed to search, retrieve, capture, and present digital information. To empower users, library staff develop transparent support systems, provide customizable access to information, and facilitate interconnectivity of information sources. They also broaden the reach of information resources by developing and presenting community programs and exhibitions.

Strategy A. Instruction

Offer an instructional program that enables students, faculty, and staff to make effective use of information resources.

- In partnership with faculty, implement the new First-Year Seminar curricular guidelines to ensure that all first-year students receive an introduction to information sources and to critical evaluation of source materials.
- Work with faculty in each academic department to integrate into the curriculum instruction for student majors in discipline-specific information research skills, strategies, and resources.
- Enhance support for individual and group learning of less-commonly taught languages. Acquire necessary technology, inform curricular decisions, and explore accredited testing options with the Office of the Dean for Academic Affairs.

Strategy B. Research support

Adapt reference services based on evolving research and instructional approaches and on changing faculty and student expectations.

- Develop, in collaboration with IT, strategies and procedures to support GIS initiatives on campus, utilizing the findings of the NITLE-funded GIS survey.
- In collaboration with the Center for Teaching and Learning, expand support for English Speakers of Other Languages (ESOL) and international students.

Folke Bernadotte Memorial Library

Strategic Plan, 2009

May 2009

Strategic Plan, 2009
Folke Bernadotte Memorial Library

Contents

1

Section One

Description And Goals

1.1 Mission, Vision, & Goals

Mission

The library advances the teaching mission and intellectual life of the College by selecting and facilitating access to information and by instructing in its use, interpretation, and evaluation.

Vision

The library will play an essential role in engaging students in critical inquiry and developing the skills and dispositions of life-long learners, prepared for lives of leadership and service in a diverse and fast-changing world. To do this, the library will support the curriculum with materials and opportunities for course-related and independent learning; will provide leadership in fostering information literacy across the curriculum; will inform the community of emerging issues in information policy and trends; and will support the intellectual and cultural life of the college by developing programs, collections, and an engaging physical and virtual space for exploration.

Goals

- Enhance the library's ability to support academic programs and students' life-long learning through adding staff and funding for improved access to collections, both print and electronic.
- Develop, preserve and promote accessible special collections and archives as a learning resource, for outreach to alumni and donors, and as a record of our institutional memory.
- Enhance the library's learning spaces and integrate them with other campus resources.
- Work toward making the library an intrinsic part of the intellectual and cultural life of the college.

1.2 Programs

The library supports the curriculum by building collections and providing research assistance and instruction to support academic programs and to serve general education and the liberal arts mission of the college. These are some of the ways we do that:

2

Strategic Plan, 2009
Folke Bernadotte Memorial Library

- Instruction: The library faculty offer various means of supporting learning. These include course-related instruction as well as a spring term course, Information Fluency. An initiative piloted in Fall 2008 developed a lab section taught by a librarian for a methods course, a model that was both innovative and remarkably successful. The librarians also see the reference desk (physical and virtual) as a site of instruction. The archives also provide instruction for classes and one-on-one opportunities for developing research skills. And for independent learning, the library provides material through its website that enable students to find resources by subject or by course. There is also a general tutorial introducing library research, information on how to cite sources, and a menu of research and technical tips. Librarians also teach courses in the first term seminar and January term programs and have been active in faculty development initiatives.
- Liaison program: Each librarian works with several departments to provide instruction and build appropriate collections.
- Assessment: Since 1998 the library has conducted annual assessments of student learning outcomes and has found those informative for our practice. We also assess our collections and services for departments as they are reviewed every ten years.
- College and Church Archives: the archives supports the curriculum, but also serves the college's administration through preserving its records and making information available to a variety of offices (the President's office, the office of the Provost, Alumni, Admissions, etc.) and to the general public.

1.3 Support Relationships

The closest support relationship for the library is between the library and the faculty, formalized in our liaison program but also enacted through myriad informal relationships. We also work closely with the Kendall Center on faculty development and student research initiatives, with Advancement (including the Grants and Foundations office), with Institutional Research, and with Gustavus Technology Services, which has a position that in part is devoted to specialized support of the library's technology needs. The College and Church Archives works closely with a wide variety of administrative offices as well as with students and faculty. The library also benefits from the work of a national award-winning friends group, the Gustavus Library Associates, which supports not only the library's acquisitions (this year providing about a quarter of all acquisitions funding through gifts and endowment) but also promotes literature and literacy. We rely on financial aid provided to students to fund wages for the approximately 100 student employees without whom we would be unable to function.

The library also has a number of important external relationships. These include several library consortia, the most important of which are Minitex, PALS, the OCLC Online Computer Library Center, and the Oberlin Group of liberal arts college libraries.

3

ection Two
Strategic Review

2.1 Strategic Issues

This section of our planning document uses the 2004 Standards for Libraries in Higher Education from the Association of College and Research Libraries to organize our analysis of the current situation. The standards address libraries' successes in planning and assessment, services, instruction, resources, access, staff, facilities, communication, administration, and budget.

2.1.1. Planning, Assessment, and Outcomes Assessment

The library has an unusual collegial management structure that has been in place for the past ten years. It has provided a solid structure for planning that is inclusive and sensitive to the needs of the Gustavus community and its institutional goals. Arising partly out of a need to address issues raised in the library's 1994 external review, we adapted the collegial structure of an academic department to the library setting. Our 2003 external review found that it worked well, particularly for the librarians; its benefits were less pronounced for the non-librarian staff (administrative and hourly). Still, all library staff and faculty are involved in planning and assessment through regular meetings, an inclusive committee structure, and annual learning outcomes assessments. The unorthodox structure was tested by the tornado of 1998, but that disaster provided an opportunity for librarians and staff members to work together in new roles. The liaison program, which developed at the same time as our internal organizational structure, has provided a healthy link with departments. We have used the departmental links to the library both as a means of communication with departments and as a sounding board, such as when we invited a consultant to review our support for the sciences in 2000.

> *Comments from Faculty, 2003*
>
> *"The somewhat unique governance structure adopted by the librarians since the last external review has had many beneficial results in efficiency, budget, and morale." (humanities division)*
>
> *"The college is fortunate to have such expert and collegial a group of librarians and staff. They do a great job within the budgetary constraints we all face." (sciences division)*

4

Strategic Plan, 2009
Folke Bernadotte Memorial Library

The college asked departments to develop <u>assessment plans</u> ten years ago. We agreed on a core set of learning outcomes and developed measures we could use to assess them. We have used that plan to guide assessment activities for the past ten years, and annually hold a retreat to review our findings. In addition to those regular assessment activities, the library faculty's scholarly work in part focuses on the scholarship of teaching and learning, resulting in a number of published studies and presentations based on our students' research and writing practices. These scholarly inquiries have enhanced our understanding of learning outcomes. We are also taking advantage of national assessments. This year with financial support from the Provost's office we joined in a <u>new national assessment</u> of information literacy especially well-adapted to liberal arts institutions made available through a NITLE/HEDS initiative. We have also been involved in the planning stages of a <u>national project</u> that promises to be the largest study ever conducted of information literacy in higher education.

In addition to measures outlined in our assessment plan, we assess our collections and services for departments by developing reports for every department and program under review annually, so that every ten years we will have assessed the entire collection and the instructional support that the library provides. We also review periodical subscriptions with departments every few years and from time to time examine standing orders and database subscriptions. Though these evaluations are not entirely outcomes-based, they do provide us an opportunity to examine our resources in terms of changing curricular needs.

Our 2003 external reviewers called our assessment techniques "excellent;" our assessment plan and activities were also singled out during the college's most recent Higher Learning Commission visit for commendation.

It is also worth mentioning that all of the recommendations made in our 1998 strategic plan that could be initiated by the library through hard work and/or redeploying parts of the library budget have been accomplished. Most of the facilities recommendations (with the significant exception of improving storage for the archives) were implemented during tornado recovery. The recommendations that would require increasing the library's budget have not been accomplished.

2.1.2 Services

The ACRL standards state that the library "should establish, promote, maintain, and evaluate a range of quality services that support the institution's mission and goals." Both of our external reviews (1993 and 2003) have praised the quality and extent of services the library offers and point out that outputs are much higher than inputs (e.g. compared to other institutions, the quality and extent of services is especially high given our unusually small staff). Surveys of faculty, students, and alumni conducted for our most recent external review showed high satisfaction with library services. Ratings of the quality of library services rose in the latest reported Senior Survey (2007) from 79% reporting it to be "good" or "very good" to 88%. Among the units included in that question, only the Marketplace had a higher rating for service than the library.

5

2.1.3 Instruction

The library has a nationally-recognized profile for innovative instructional programs that rests on foundations laid in previous generations. In the 1950s the library director emphasized the teaching role of the library, a function that was not widely recognized at other institutions until the 1970s, which is when our library formalized its instructional role by hiring its first coordinator of instructional programs. Our two previous external reviews praised our instruction efforts. The 2003 reviewers pointed out that the amount of course-related instruction we provide exceeds the Oberlin Group average by a "significant amount" and cautioned that "there are simply not enough librarians to continue to grow in the area of instruction and simultaneously to carry on their many other responsibilities." Given the institution's emphasis on student learning, and the importance of information literacy in a liberal education, we feel this is an essential purpose for the library and do not plan to scale our efforts back.

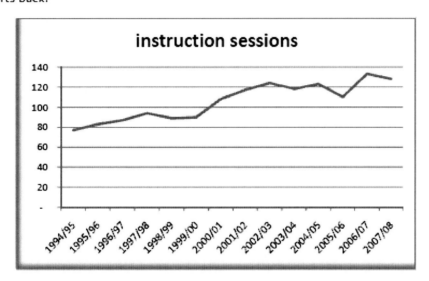

In addition to one-on-one tutorial assistance at the reference desk and in the archives – both important sites of learning for our students – we provide course-related instruction for over 120 courses each year, reaching over 2,000 students annually. These workshops focus on resources and research strategies tied to particular assignments and may involve one to three meetings with a class. The archivist provides both group and one-on-one instruction in the use of archival materials in connection with courses and projects. We also provide online and printed guides to resources by subject area for students who prefer independent exploration.

Strategic Plan, 2009
Folke Bernadotte Memorial Library

We also teach some credit-bearing courses each year. For the past five years, we have offered a .5 credit 300-level interdisciplinary course in the spring semester for students who are going on to graduate study or who simply want to know more about research. Though enrollment is limited to fit into the library's small seminar classroom space, the student evaluations have been very positive. We also make an effort to contribute a course to the first term seminar program and to support Curriculum II as well teaching January term courses and overseeing independent studies and career explorations.

An innovation this fall was for one of the librarians (Julie Gilbert) to teach a "lab section" – one hour a week of a course meeting four hours weekly – of a 200-level methods course in political science. This was a successful melding of the philosophy behind course-related instruction with a deeper commitment to the more complex skills involved in information literacy that are beyond the scope of typical library sessions. This was a demonstrable success and will be continued this spring. We will be seeking ways to enable more partnerships like this, though our current staffing levels may make that difficult.

> *Comments from faculty,*
> *2003*
>
> *"Librarians are wonderful at teaching the necessary skills, both on an individual basis and in the classroom."*
> *(fine arts division)*

Faculty development is another area in which librarians have contributed to the College's instructional mission. In 1999 the library received a $79,000 National Leadership Grant from the federal Institute of Museum and Library Services to develop a model librarian/faculty collaboration to enhance developmental research skills in a hybrid print/electronic environment. This grant enabled us to host two regional librarians' institutes and to hold two summer workshops for our faculty, who designed or redesigned courses to embed in them developmental research skills. Results from the grant were disseminated through conference presentations and publications as well as invited workshops at other colleges. We remain the only liberal arts college library to ever receive a research and demonstration grant from this federal agency.

The library has also contributed to the most recent summer workshop offered by the Kendall Center, to FTS training workshops, and to various other faculty development programs. This January, thanks to support from the Kendall Center, we were able to involve ten faculty in a shortened and adapted version of our 300-level course in a three-day workshop on "How Information Works."

Comparatively, we do a lot of teaching. Of the 13 Oberlin Group colleges with endowments of under $110 million, only one of those libraries reached more students in instruction sessions than we did in 2007/08. Though we don't have comparative statistics for credit-bearing courses, our contributions to FTS, CII, and January Term are unusual and almost certainly much higher than at any of our comparison schools.

7

2.1.4 Resources

The ACRL standards for resources address two dimensions: how many resources are provided by the library and how well the library manages its allocation of resources. We do very poorly on the first measure and much better on the second. Inadequate funding for acquisitions requires that we work closely with faculty across the campus to make good choices. Being short-staffed also requires a constant attention to priority-setting. While many faculty feel the library fails to provide adequate resources for the areas in which they teach, they seem to feel their share of an inadequate pie is at least equitable and that we do the best we can to make decisions transparently and collaboratively.

2.1.5 Staff

On many measures, our staff is outstanding. The rigors of full faculty status (and its rewards) involve librarians in teaching, scholarship, and service of a high standard. The administrative and hourly staff are dedicated, innovative, and committed to the institution. We take full advantage of opportunities for professional development and, within the limited resources of the library's budget, provide funds for non-faculty staff development using a formula similar to that for faculty travel to conferences.

On the other hand, we could do much more if we had an adequate level of staffing. Our past two external reviews commented on the disconnect between the numbers of staff and their output. In the words of the 1993 reviewers, the college "gets a lot of bang for its buck." In 2003, the reviewers said "despite a huge workload, [the librarians] are remarkable in their energy and enthusiasm." Comparatively, we are significantly understaffed.

> *Comments from faculty, 2003*
>
> *"The professional librarians are excellent resources for students and faculty, the liaison program is well-received by departments, and the library itself is an excellent site for research and learning. Very impressive." (education division)*
>
> *"I have never seen a more dedicated and effective staff at a library. It is truly a model for what a liberal arts college library should be." (fine arts division)*
>
> *"Reference people are great!! Calm, relaxed, willing to help." (social sciences division)*

When looking at the ratio of library staff (faculty, administrative, and hourly) per student at the 12 Oberlin Group libraries that have endowments of less than $110 million, Gustavus has the fewest staff per student. Or to put it differently, we each have more students to serve than at any of the other libraries. Seven of these colleges have smaller endowments than ours. The data has been anonymized in compliance with our statistics sharing agreement, but it's safe to say that these are not schools generally considered superior to Gustavus.

8

Strategic Plan, 2009
Folke Bernadotte Memorial Library

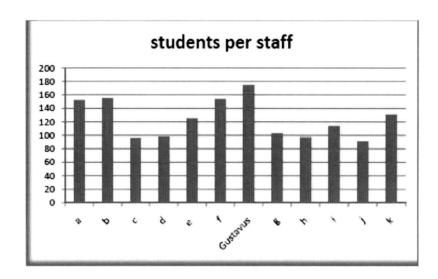

The college and church archives are also understaffed. A consultant whose visit was funded by a Preservation Assistance Grant from the National Endowment for the Humanities in 2006 recommended that within the next year the college administration "should review the college's commitment to the archival and artifactual collections, as more staff time and additional funding is absolutely necessary." As Edi Thorstensson retires from the part-time Church Archivist position, the staffing shortage will only worsen.

2.1.6 Facilities

A 1965 document outlining what a new library building should look like presciently stated the emphasis was "more on *student* learning and less on *faculty* teaching." We are grateful to those who planned the present library building and to the staff who maintain it. It has remained a remarkably flexible, hospitable space, and renovations following the 1998 tornado provided both a more sensible layout for the collections and a chance to update furniture and carpeting both in the main library and the Lund Music/Speech library.

That said, both the main library and the music branch are experiencing serious space issues. The main library was designed to hold 300,000 volumes before an addition would be needed, which at the time the building was designed expected to occur in the 1990s. In part, the need for an addition has been delayed because annual collection growth has diminished. In 1965 10,000 volumes were being added annually and, according to the report of that year, "there is no reason to believe this rate will not increase." In fact, in the past 5 years, we have averaged less than half that number.

9

The cost of periodicals and databases increases at least 10% annually.

-

There are rising expectations among faculty who are engaging in more student/faculty research than in the past and who expect – and are required – to be professionally engaged in their own scholarship.

-

There is a greater output of both printed and electronic materials. In spite of pronouncements that books are dead, the number of books published in the last decade has doubled; the numbers of databases on offer increases constantly, as do demands to provide electronic access to the increasing amounts of research in the subjects we teach.

-

Electronic journals are bundled into expensive packages that can change overnight both in contents and in price.

-

The consolidation of publishing industries leaves more publications in fewer hands; parent corporations often demand higher profit margins and increase costs to libraries. The instability of current/traditional publishing models leaves us vulnerable to the possibility of critical parts of the information industries failing altogether.

Though collection growth has been slower than expected, we have reached capacity for collections and are planning an ambitious effort to evaluate and remove outdated books. (We have already been aggressively weeding our journals collection by removing those for which we have stable electronic access.) We also recognize that the facility is heavily used by students for individual and group study and at times our study spaces approach saturation.

The archives is also in need of more and better space. We need more room for storage of materials, more appropriate shelving, and better environmental controls. According the NEH-funded consultant, the college and church archives "are in desperate need for more storage space and additional practical work space."

Under strategic initiatives we will describe some recommendations for changes in facilities to address these issues.

2.1.7 Communication and cooperation

The library has made strides since our 1993 external review on communication both within and beyond the library. We have built strong relationships with faculty through our liaison program. Within the library we have regularized a committee structure and regular all-staff meetings and share budget information, decision-making, and planning. We are using Web 2.0 technologies such as a blog, RSS feeds, and social bookmarking to add to more traditional means of communication. A new committee on outreach and promotion, formed in 2008, is seeking regular ways to enhance communication with the community and to tap into campus-wide initiatives.

2.1.8 Administration

According to ACRL standards, "the library should be administered in a manner that permits and encourages the most effective use of library resources." We feel our inclusive and collaborative structure, coupled with a high degree of individual commitment to the mission of the library and the college, accomplishes that.

2.1.9 Budget

Some of the ACRL standards language on budget deals with how well a library prepares, administers, and monitors its budget. We feel we accomplish those tasks well. Sylvia Straub, in particular, deserves credit for monitoring our complex budget throughout the year.

10

Strategic Plan, 2009
Folke Bernadotte Memorial Library

However, in answer to a key questions raised in the ACRL standards, "are the library's annual authorized expenditures adequate to meet the ongoing, appropriate needs of the library?" the answer is, quite bluntly, no.

A faculty survey conducted for our 2003 external review showed that faculty felt quite strongly that the library will continue to be an essential resource on campus in future. They did not believe that the library provides the resources students need or sufficient support for faculty research needs, though many added parenthetically that this was due to limited funding, not poor management of resources.

This concern was not limited to any one division. Access to journal literature is a perennial sore spot with faculty across campus. Even though we have access to more electronic journals, they come in packages that don't necessarily match our curricular needs.

We are spending an increasing amount of money on copyright fees to pay for access to articles that we obtain through interlibrary loan that fall outside of fair use provisions. Each calendar year, an institution may only obtain five articles published within the most recent five years from any one journal. Beyond that use we must pay a fee that is often as high as the price of a book. Articles obtained through interlibrary loan, even when permissions are paid, are only for individual use and cannot be used in a class or placed on Moodle. Interlibrary loan is meant to be the exception, not the rule. According to our agreement with Minitex, our library must supply at least 95% of our local needs. If we begin to rely too heavily on interlibrary loan, we will run the risk of losing access to it altogether.

Comparatively, our library is underfunded. When looking at acquisitions expenditures per student among the 13 Oberlin Group institutions with endowments of less than $110 million, Gustavus ranks dead last.

Copyright law changes made in 1998 have pushed materials out of the public domain and will keep newer publications out of the public domain far longer than previously; an increasing number of works will be "orphaned" – without anyone to provide permission for use; digital materials are protected under terms that limit fair use. A brewing legal dispute between libraries and publishers over electronic reserves may lead to restrictions on current practices that could lead to much higher costs to libraries, students, or both.

–

Every year, a greater percentage of our budget goes to electronic resources that we don't own and which will disappear if we fail to pay high annual subscription fees that increase annually at double-digit rates.

–

An external review of our support for the science departments in 2000 concluded our access to research materials is inadequate and "an overall increase in the library budget is the only solution. This may take a few years to accomplish, and probably will, but Gustavus needs to adopt this philosophy in order to maintain a quality science program." Our budget since that external review has decreased by over $50,000.

11

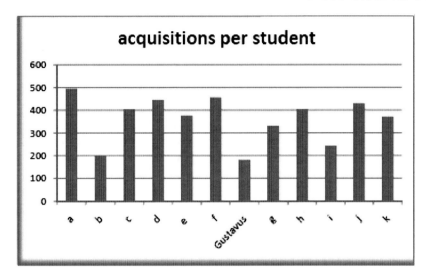

Our acquisitions budget, a mix of funds from the college's operational budget and from restricted endowments and gifts, has not only failed to keep up with cost increases, it has shrunk. Our budget has declined by 12% since 2002, while expenses rise. This is unusual among institutions with comparable endowments.

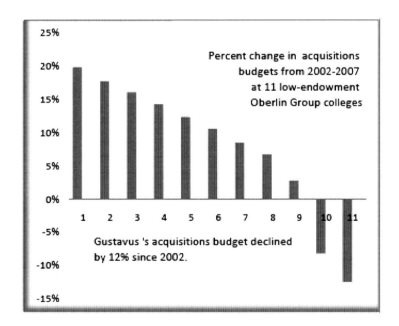

12

Strategic Plan, 2009

Folke Bernadotte Memorial Library

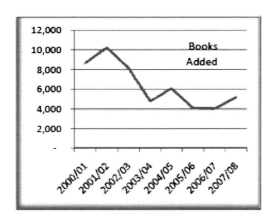

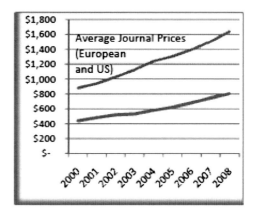

Our ability to add books has declined since the price of subscriptions to periodicals and online databases increase steeply every year, from 10 – 15% annually. Even when we cut journal subscriptions, as we have done frequently, we can't make up enough ground to do more than maintain what's left. The chart below shows what the library's budget would look like if we had increased our 1998 total budget (not including wages and benefits) by 5% or 3% annually. The bottom line is our actual budget.

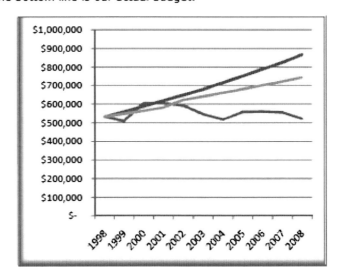

To summarize our strengths, weaknesses, opportunities and challenges, we have the imagination, the energy, and the commitment that it takes to have an excellent library. In this rapidly-changing information environment, the kind of learning we promote is needed more than ever. We are pleased that AAC&U recognizes this and includes information literacy in its list of "essential outcomes." We have developed a national profile for doing this well, and are contributing to the professional discourse by engaging in the scholarship of teaching and learning in this area.

13

But we face a grave weakness in funding for staff and collections and face pressing challenges in providing access to information needed to support our programs because of high and constantly increasing costs. Without increases to our budget that match increasing costs, we are forced to either stop buying books and videos, cut subscriptions to journals and databases, or both.

2.2 Barriers

We have excellent relations with faculty across the disciplines, a general belief within the community that the library matters, and a pleasant and well-used facility. Our friends group, Gustavus Library Associates, provides a national model for fund-raising and support. Our instruction program has a strong national profile. But still, funding for staff and collections is a huge barrier. Every dollar our friends raise is used as budget relief, and even so we've seen our budget shrink in recent years. Though the staff has boundless energy and imagination, we can only do so much without financial support. And with such a lean staff, we cannot engage in initiatives that would enhance our programs and are stretched to the limit to sustain what we currently do. If we are forced to cut acquisitions further, as we almost certainly will in the coming months, it will have a harmful impact on faculty recruitment and retention. Student/faculty research opportunities will suffer, and our best students will be underprepared for graduate work.

Externally, the uncertain economy, keeping up with changes in the information landscape, challenges facing the information industries as they transition to a digital future, and the rising costs of materials are all barriers. So is copyright law that has reduced the public domain and fair use and criminalizes use of cultural materials that might fall outside the fuzzy four factors test of fair use. As state funding is reduced, we also may lose access to databases funded by the state (Academic Search Premier being the most important of those) and the contributions made by state funding to consortial subscriptions to databases and electronic journal collections. In 2008, Minitex estimates it provided over $360,000 in materials and subsidies to Gustavus, primarily for electronic databases. The governor has recommended a minimum of a 10% cut in the Minitex budget; it may turn out to be a deeper cut, depending on the state of the economy.

Lack of funding for school libraries, inequitable access to broadband Internet access, disparity among school districts, and the emphasis placed by NCLB on teaching to the test are barriers for our instruction efforts. We no longer can assume, for example, that students have ever been introduced to the idea of using a book's index to locate specific information or that they can interpret a citation. We also recognize that most students are less skilled at finding information for academic purposes on the Internet than their confidence levels would indicate.

Strategic Plan, 2009
Folke Bernadotte Memorial Library

Section Three
Strategic Initiatives

Goal 1. Enhance the library's ability to support academic programs and students' life-long learning through adding staff and funding for improved access to collections, both print and electronic.

1.1: Increase and enhance library staffing

1.1.1 Provide a career path within the library for non-faculty library staff. To do this, we would like to see the establishment of ranks (library specialist I, II, III, and IV) so that employees who continue to grow in their professional responsibilities can be recognized and rewarded without having to take a different position. Under this new system, previous relevant experience would be acknowledged at point of hire. Thereafter, to advance from one rank to another, staff would submit a detailed portfolio of their professional work to be evaluated against pre-established guidelines. A committee of peers (librarians and library staff) would determine whether the individual should be advanced to a higher rank and would make a recommendation to the Provost. Advancement would carry with it an increased salary. This system would provide opportunities for growth, recognition of excellence, increased flexibility within positions, and meaningful accountability.

1.1.2 Design a high degree of flexibility into all staff positions so that staff responsibilities can continually adapt to meet new needs. While all staff would continue to have areas of specialization, they would also share some responsibilities (with cross-training where appropriate) and be able to work together on projects and tasks.

1.1.3 Make sufficient resources available to provide non-faculty library staff with professional development opportunities and the time and financial support for engagement with state and national initiatives.

Links to the College's Strategic Plan

Enhance Gustavus academic strength in student-centered learning in the liberal arts disciplines and pre-professional education by investing in academic departments and programs.

-

Develop more fully and staff appropriately a program of undergraduate research and creativity across the curriculum.

-

Develop and implement a robust model of lifelong learning that is firmly rooted in our liberal arts tradition and consonant with our academic and co-curricular programs.

-

Set competitive compensation goals for staff, faculty, and administrators informed by appropriate budget models and timeframes by which to meet these goals.

-

Engage in ongoing strategic planning throughout the College in a manner linked to responsible resource management.

15

1.1.4 Bring in a consultant to conduct a workflow analysis within the next three years. This consultancy (possibly provided by R2, a consulting firm that has been used successfully by several peer institutions) will enable the library to examine current practices, recommend ways to streamline processes, and advise the library on ways to manage both print and electronic resources. The ultimate hope is that it will create space for pursuing new projects and allow us to take a more deliberate, less reactive, approach to electronic resources management. Such a consultancy could also advise us on efficient and effective ways to weed the collection, a task that is urgent since we have reached the building's capacity for print collections.

1.1.5 Upgrade the administrative coordinator/budget manager position following the recommendation made in our 2003 external review which stated it was "probably one of the most important positions in light of the new organizational model. If this style of organizational management continues, it is important to have this business manager elevated to administrative status."

1.1.6 Add positions to provide room for innovation. Faculty positions would have an area of specialization while also teaching, serving as a liaison to departments, providing reference services, and participating in collegial management of the library. Staff positions would include student employee supervision, service on library committees, and participation in library planning and development. The specializations for these new positions should be:

- Faculty position specializing in outreach, promotion, and programming. Responsibilities would include serving as liaison to the Gustavus Library Associates; coordinating support of academic summer programs; planning library programs that complement campus initiatives; coordinating library-related faculty development and relationships with student affairs and the Diversity Center.

- Faculty position specializing in Web development. Responsibilities would include providing leadership in developing an accessible and standards-compliant website, integrating the catalog and other databases into the website and course management systems through RSS feeds and adapting other Web 2.0 developments to the library setting; integrating new digital formats into our online collections, and assisting with migration of audio-visual formats to digital access.

- Faculty position for scholarly communications. Responsibilities would include serving as a copyright resource for the faculty, advising the campus on ways of using digital and print resources in scholarly and creative work without violating copyright, assisting with the development of an institutional repository for student and faculty work, and encouraging open access to scholarly work.

- Staff position (full time) for archives and special collections. Responsibilities would include work involving the arrangement, description, evaluation, and preservation and rehabilitation of historical materials; digitization of paper and photographic

16

Strategic Plan, 2009
Folke Bernadotte Memorial Library

records; assistance locating archival information; and training and supervision of student employees. [Note: we have requested a 12 month half-time position]

- Staff position (full time) to manage the music library. Responsibilities would include supervision of student employees and collections, keeping up with trends in music librarianship, including digital and streaming alternatives to analog audio collections, and keeping the library abreast of intellectual property issues as they pertain to music. [Note: there is currently no position assigned to this library; when a half-time employee retired, the work of that position was absorbed by staff in the main library.]

1.2 Improve collections and enhance access

1.2.3 Add funding, with annual increases, to support the purchase of resources needed for our programs and to enhance their management and access. This will aid in recruitment and retention of the faculty and students who we want at Gustavus and will alleviate the persistent need to cut journals, databases, and book allocations just to balance our budget. It will also enhance our ability to support student and faculty research by making the library's resources more seamlessly accessible.

1.2.4 Support the regular evaluation of collections by using OCLC's WorldCat Collection Analysis tool every 3-5 years, engaging in a regularized weeding program, and examining use statistics for our print and electronic collections.

1.2.5 Integrate library resources more effectively with the campus Course Management System. We should seek ways to feed relevant materials via RSS to course pages and draw students from their course pages to library resources, enhancing these "walled gardens" in ways that will encourage students to explore beyond the core course content.

1.2.6 Create an effective documentation system for electronic resource management to identify, maintain, and (where necessary) create documentation for electronic resource management, including policies, procedures, and workflows. The documentation should be accessible to library faculty and staff and to patrons, when appropriate. This initiative will reduce duplicate, outdated, and hidden documentation, and make our electronic resources management program more transparent and efficient.

1.2.7 Acquire an effective electronic resource management system (ERMS) to assist us in managing the details of our subscriptions, from licensing terms to usage statistics. We will explore a range of ERMS options, from commercial products, to open source software, to locally developed databases and spreadsheets. While we ideally would like to coordinate all of our electronic content in one system, we may find it best to use alternate systems for certain types of information. For instance, it may be that ERMS software works well for databases, while a separate module is best for individual e-journals that we manage through our subscription agent. Developing an effective ERMS not only involves identifying tools with which to manage our subscriptions, but implementing an effective system for

17

communicating information about those subscriptions to library faculty and staff and, in some cases, teaching them to use the ERMS themselves.

1.2.8 Advance seamless access to electronic resources and the systems we use to support them. We will explore ways to provide our patrons with more seamless access to electronic content through a variety of tools, from database interfaces, to the online catalog, to link resolvers, to federated (one-stop) search tools, to the library's web site, to the course management system. We will continue to investigate emerging developments in catalogs, including open source options, and the emerging expectation that cell phones will become a standard access tool for Internet-based information. (According to the Pew Internet & American Life Project, "the mobile device will be the primary connection tool to the internet for most people in the world in 2020.") Our hope is not only to advance access to learning resources for patrons, but also to promote better integration of the internal systems that our library faculty and staff use to manage them, from our ERM systems, to our web page authoring environment, to our online catalog staff modules, to our systems for tracking budgets.

1.3 Support use of new information formats with enhanced staffing and the addition of equipment, software, and materials (datasets, visual resources, audio collections, poster printers, etc.) to enable students to become adept at using new information formats such as geographic information systems, video production, poster design, and to provide expertise in the technical, legal, and intellectually effective use of these materials. Currently the library is not able to support the most basic traditional needs of the college, much less venture into emerging forms of expression. We have pockets of expertise on campus. The geography department currently is the only department with resources for combining spatial information and data – but geographic information systems are useful for all fields and are an increasingly important form of information analysis. Video production is another form of intellectual expression that currently is only supported within one department. All students would benefit from having the opportunity to create scholarly projects in video format. And as students are increasingly presenting their research in the form of poster presentations, the means to do so should be more readily available during hours that are more convenient for students. The library would be the logical place for all of these emerging technologies to be put in play. (To frame it differently, not having them in the library would be like providing access to computers only for students in the Mathematics and Computer Science department, as once was the case.) The library could then become the center not just for information literacy involving traditional forms of information but for visual and media literacy.

Goal 2: Develop, preserve and promote accessible special collections and archives as a learning resource, for outreach to alumni and donors, and as a record of our institutional memory.

2.1 Follow up on the recommendations made by the NEH consultant concerning the urgent need to upgrade resources in terms of staff, space, and environmental controls. The archivist needs time and resources to review needs and create a comprehensive collections

18

Strategic Plan, 2009
Folke Bernadotte Memorial Library

management policy in order to work with campus constituents to regularize and formalize accession and preservation of materials.

2.2 Evaluate special collections with the aim of building a collection appropriate for our curriculum that is also visible (most likely by relocating it to the main floor where security and accessibility would be better balanced). Develop instructional uses for both special collections and archives. Integrate the use of these collections, where appropriate, into courses across the curriculum.

2.3 Consider grant sources for conservation, preservation, and digitization projects.

2.4 Invest in a robust online repository system such as OCLC's CONTENTdm so that archival materials can be digitized and shared with the campus and the world. This would be particularly valuable for promotion of the college's 150th anniversary, for classroom teaching, and for outreach to alumni, donors, and scholars, and could be valuable for other programs, as described below.

2.5 Complete digitization of the *Gustavian Weekly* (currently only available for the years 1980 – 2005) for preservation and for use by students, alumni, and researchers.

Goal 3: Enhance the library's learning spaces and integrate them with other campus resources.

3.1 Plan an addition to the library in conjunction with other building projects (e.g. the new Social Sciences building and the renovation of Anderson) so that features that would be more effectively situated in the library are not preemptively placed in other buildings without evaluating best placement in future. Consider bringing in a consultant, such as Scott Bennett, to inform discussions early in the planning process.

3.2 Provide security for the music library's collections. Currently our branch library lacks the security measures available in the main library, which has led to significant losses.

3.3 Increase and improve group and individual study spaces and include space for faculty development programming and high-end technology experimentation.

3.4 Provide a new space for special collections on the main floor – perhaps by relocating the contents of the microfilm area and building locked shelving to house our rare books in a visible and accessible but secure location. Create space for reception, research, and instruction in the archives.

3.5 Increase the number and convenient placement of electrical outlets. The 1965 plan for the new library building commented that "libraries never have enough outlets." That statement is even more true as students bring laptops to the library for extended periods of work. Our furniture has been migrating toward the scarce outlets on pillars and walls as students seek power for their laptops.

19

Links to the College's Strategic Plan

Build and renovate academic facilities in a manner informed by the curriculum, student needs, and environmental stewardship.

-

Enhance Gustavus's strength in student-centered learning through a strong partnership between the Divisions of Student Affairs and Academic Affairs.

-

Ensure access to the critical support services needed to ensure students have the opportunity to achieve their fullest potential.

-

Increase engagement with our alumni to enable them to actively advance and engage in the mission of the College.

-

Enhance student engagement through the development of residential learning communities to integrate student learning beyond the classroom.

-

Develop and sustain a community committed to and practiced in intellectual diversity and civil discourse.

3.6 Provide a 24/7 study space for students that can be part of the library during regular library hours, but restricted after hours. When students complain that the library has insufficient hours, they are really seeking space that is conducive for study, not for access to the print collections.

3.7 Consider housing GTS in the enhanced library. Media services, technical support, instructional support, etc. could all benefit from proximity to the library staff and library users as well as to one another.

3.8 Include a café in the library to encourage faculty presence in the library and the kinds of accidental conversations that happen in places where good coffee and books are available.

3.9 Include a flexible learning commons space that integrates resources and services for students working individually and in groups. Incorporate flexible dividers so that varying amounts of the space can be set aside for classes using technology. Ensure that there are seminar-style tables for discussion as well as computer stations.

3.10 Consider locating allied student and faculty services in the library as appropriate – academic advising, the Writing Center, the Kendall Center, tutoring services, disability services, the Diversity Center, etc.

Goal 4: Work toward making the library an intrinsic part of the intellectual and cultural life of the college.

4.1 The library is well positioned to foster an understanding of emerging issues in information policies and trends in collaboration with faculty, staff, students and the greater community. This could include programming in coordination with the Kendall Center and GTS to enhance the use of emerging technologies in teaching and learning. The library could also serve as a clearinghouse and "early warning system" for changes in the information industries and intellectual property law and legislation. The library could also assist faculty in their participation in the open access movement to increase both the visibility of their scholarship and the profile of the college. The NIH initiative and the Harvard Arts and Sciences faculty vote to deposit their scholarship online are

20

Strategic Plan, 2009
Folke Bernadotte Memorial Library

indications that the <u>open access</u> movement, properly supported, will lead to new and less expensive ways to make research accessible.

4.2 The library is the common ground for the campus, and we should make use of it to promote the appreciation of cultural expression as well as for enhancing students' inclination to become engaged in the world. This is work that can be presented in both physical and virtual formats, but will require additional staff, enough space, and the technical facility to do this work effectively.

4.3 With additional staff and funding, the library could create a repository for a wide variety of expression. Such a repository (already described in 2.4, above) could host material from the college archives and special collections to make them available to the wider world, could showcase exemplary student work, could serve as a public gateway for the Hillstrom Museum and other programs that have cultural materials to share, and could be a digital space where faculty could deposit those scholarly and pedagogical materials that they wish to make accessible. Accessibility would depend not just on providing the server and software, but appropriate metadata and organization.

4.4 Designate time and space for collaborative research and exploration among library staff to enhance our instructional goals, use of our collections, and our sharing of what we learn with the wider world. This creative activity will enable us to better support our patrons in our daily work and participate more deliberately in discussions on issues ranging from the implementation of new educational technology on campus, to the creation of an institutional repository, to the identification of gifting opportunities, to the implications of intellectual property and scholarly communication issues, to joint efforts among libraries to better integrate the systems we use for access and discovery and our instructional collaborations with faculty across campus.

ection Four
Assessment

We will use a combination of input, output, and outcomes measures to assess whether we have reached the goals spelled out in this document.

Goal 1: Enhance the library's ability to support academic programs and students' life-long learning through adding staff and funding for improved access to collections, both print and electronic. Success will mean having a sufficient budget that increases regularly to keep up with rising costs, additional staff lines, a new way of evaluating and promoting staff to reward professional growth throughout a staff member's career, more instructional programs in collaboration with faculty in the disciplines, more forms of information such as datasets and visual resources as well as the ability to use them in instruction, and improved student learning as demonstrated through our assessment plan measures.

Goal 2: Develop, preserve and promote accessible special collections and archives as a learning resource, for outreach to alumni and donors, and as a record of our institutional memory. Success will mean having a larger, more secure facility, enough staff to curate and process collections, a digitization program for appropriate records, a public repository for appropriate materials, special collections that are more visible and integrated into the curriculum, and a common understanding of the role of the archives and what decisions need to be made for records management, digital assets management, and the preservation of historically significant documents. Outcomes will include enhanced engagement with constituents both on and off campus, greater alumni awareness of the college and its assets, and improved student learning.

Goal 3: Enhance the library's learning spaces and integrate them with other campus resources. Success will mean having an expanded library that allows for more and better learning spaces as well as the presence of student and faculty services that would benefit by being located in the library and an increase in the number of visits. Outcomes will include measurements of greater student engagement with research and creative activities as well as improved satisfaction with the facility.

Goal 4: Work toward making the library an intrinsic part of the intellectual and cultural life of the college. Success will mean having more and better dialogues with faculty and students on cultural and intellectual issues, more programs identified with the library, more exhibits in the library, and a well-organized institutional repository that will be visited and will enhance Gustavus's institutional profile. Outcomes will be a higher level of student engagement with cultural and social issues as measured in the Senior Survey, NSSE senior data, focus groups, department reviews, etc.

Northern Kentucky University

W. Frank Steely Library

Strategic Plan

Mission

Steely Library partners with its users in their quest for information—through access, through innovation, and through its people.

Vision

We seek to become the information resource of first choice for the NKU community and to be a noted center for excellence in our collections relating to the history and heritage of our region.

Key Action Areas

Curriculum
To enable our users to thrive in a world that is increasingly information-based, we must help them to develop skills to effectively find, evaluate, and use appropriate information resources.

Collections
To be the primary source of information for our users, we must provide and preserve access to the richest array of resources possible.

Public Engagement
To support the University's commitment to civic engagement, the Library and its faculty must develop opportunities for creative projects to address community needs appropriate to our expertise.

Measurement & Assessment
To ensure that we are effectively and efficiently meeting user needs, we must develop a culture of assessment and adopt appropriate tools and techniques to measure our progress.

Technology
To ensure program excellence, we will deploy state-of-the-art technology as appropriate.

Development
With the realization that state support provides the essentials and that private support is necessary to support excellence, we must expand private giving and grant funding for Steely Library's efforts.

Marketing
To ensure full utilization of Library facilities, collections, and expertise, internal and external marketing and communications must be fully integrated into the planning and operations processes.

Faculty Development
In order to meet the challenges of 21st century librarianship, we must develop a faculty body that is both prepared and engaged in the profession and the University community.

Staff Development
In order to meet the challenges and needs of the 21st century library clientele, we must enhance staff skills.

Goals and Objectives

Curriculum

Goal: Expand the focus and reach of the Steely Library Instructional Program.

Objective 1: Expand the implementation of the information literacy sequential curriculum: A Sequential Curriculum Plan @ W. Frank Steely Library, as a critical aspect of an NKU degree program and the foundation to life-long learning skills for our graduates.

Strategy A: Extend instructional presentation program to include online course sessions – live or via pre-designed instructional guides.

- RIS will investigate options such as Blackboard Librarian, online class sessions, etc. to be involved with web-based courses with information literacy instruction and research assistance.
  - Blackboard customizable course cartridges have been developed are offered for direct uploads to course instructors.
  - Online tutorials utilizing Wimba and Captivate are available for all levels and subject disciplines; additional course-specific tutorials are developed in collaboration with course instructors.

Strategy B: Create online instruction modules as a means to extend the number of NKU classes reached by our Information Literacy Sequential Curriculum and to better collaborate with instructors teaching in a web or blended environment.

Objective 2: Evaluate new avenues for teaching information literacy skills to our students, either through a standalone course or through an "across the curriculum" approach.

Strategy A: Continue to create new courses for the ongoing Bachelor of Library Informatics program.
- Pursue a second IMLS grant to expand access to scholarship program to areas of the state not targeted under the first grant.

Strategy B: Expand instructional offerings both in the fields of library and information science as well as information literacy within the other disciplines taught at NKU.

Strategy C: Provide programming in reading, library resources, and research skills development for College of Education students and working school teachers and librarians in the northern Kentucky area in support of requirements from the College of Education and the state of Kentucky for professional portfolio development.

Collections

Goal: Provide and preserve access to the richest array of information resources possible.

Objective 1: Develop strategies to optimize the mix between access and ownership of resources.

Strategy A: Continue assessing usage data to determine subscribed journal holdings and databases.

Strategy B: Further refine the procedures of information brokerage and interlibrary loan to produce one seamless process for users.

Strategy C: Investigate implementation of a federated searching tool to maximize user access to electronic resources.

Strategy D: Continue cooperative collection building through participation in FoKAL

Strategy E: Pursue digital initiatives to increase and broaden available resources.
- Examine collections in Special Collections & Archives to determine where digitization is beneficial and possible.

Objective 2: Improve the effectiveness of collection management in order to maximize resources.

Strategy A: Identify criteria for determining resources for new and continuing programs and courses.

Strategy B: Revise the Collection Policy for Special Collections & Archives and share with those people who are collecting on behalf of the department.

Public Engagement

Goal: Develop public engagement efforts both as a Library and on the part of the Steely Library faculty by actively seeking opportunities, and by facilitating and encouraging efforts by individual employees.

Objective 1: Increase the number of community engagement projects undertaken by Steely faculty and staff.

Strategy A: Communicate library priorities to faculty/staff to generate ideas for fundable projects.

Strategy B: Provide increased awareness of available grants and funding sources through e-mail announcements and other appropriate means of communication.

Strategy C: Investigate more effective means of communicating funding opportunities and funded programs/awards to faculty/staff.

Strategy D: Advertise Cash Incentive Award program.

Objective 2: Develop regular, on-going public programming events.

Strategy A: Utilize the resources available through the American Library Association's Public Programs.

Strategy B: Continue to build our partnership with the Friends of Steely Library in the funding of programs aimed at the community.

Strategy C: Investigate the best means for structuring public programming by the library.

Strategy D: Collaborate with other faculty/units on campus as appropriate on public programs.

Objective 3: Increase faculty scholarly/creative service activities that would engage the library with the surrounding community.

Strategy A: Promote and encourage faculty to apply for University-Community Partnership Grants.

Strategy B: Encourage faculty teaching a course to incorporate service learning projects into their curriculum.

Strategy C: Advertise and promote the current community service projects engaged in by the library faculty.

Measurement & Assessment

Goal: Create a culture of assessment throughout the Library.

Objective 1: Assessment Work Team will coordinate the effort to increase levels of awareness of assessment efforts.

Strategy A: Continue to refine assessment plan.

Strategy B: Investigate ways to implement a culture of assessment throughout the Library's operations.

Objective 3: In conjunction with Marketing Work Team, continue to investigate means for obtaining user feedback.

Strategy A: Review and evaluate effectiveness of suggestion boxes.

Strategy B: Continue to seek collaborative means to gather data, e.g. OPAC usability testing.

Objective 4: Optimize internal data collection within Steely Library.

Strategy A: Investigate standardization of reports generated throughout the Library.

Strategy B: Determine what data is needed and/or lacking as well as that which is no longer needed.

Strategy C: Determine what data needs to be accessible and how to best make data centrally available.

Technology

Goal: Deploy state-of-the-art technology as a support for program excellence.

Objective 1: Identify and implement technology to improve efficiency and effectiveness in managing physical collections.

Strategy A: Implement an RFID system to improve speed and accuracy of the inventory process, and to eventually allow self checkout

Strategy B: Purchase and install compact shelving in the Special Collections and Archives area and other areas where space optimization is important.

Objective 2: Update Steely Library's infrastructure to meet current standards.

Strategy A: Work with IT to identify physical wiring upgrades needed for improved access.
Strategy B: Increase server space to support increase in digital resources available to patrons

Objective 3: Improve information search capabilities to better empower Library users to find the best data to fit their needs.

Strategy A: Work with Voyager Team in revising and enhancing the Voyager OPAC.

- Continue to create alternative entry points for NKUIRE
- Create ways to add archival material [non-book material] into the OPAC

Strategy B: Work with Voyager Team to maintain usability testing for the Voyager OPAC

Strategy C: Investigate and implement new technology tools in support of the instructional mission of the Library.

Strategy D: With the formation of the Digital Initiatives Work Team in 2009, investigate the implementation of metasearching.

Objective 4: Make the Steely Library virtual presence both a more effective channel for the dissemination of Library information and a better tool for use in the Library's instructional mission.

Strategy A: Work with the Web Librarian in improving web access for portable devices (e.g. BlackBerry)
• Use web standards and accessibility guidelines to ensure greatest possible device interdependence.
• Test and validate pages regularly to ensure guidelines are followed consistently.
• Implement a template that uses a proper logical content order and a semantic structure for pages.

Strategy B: Convert parts of the site into database driven engines which can be edited via web forms.
• With the assistance of the Web Team, build parts of the site in PHP.
• With the assistance of the Web Team, create web forms so people can add   their own content, such as news, without coding.

Strategy C: Use Web Team and the Marketing Work Team to ensure content is up-to-date.
• Have Web Team members review portions of the site under their purview.
• Let Web Team approve suggested top-level changes.
• Consult with the Marketing Committee as necessary.

Strategy D: Create systems adequate to support digital collections, archives, and repositories.

Strategy E: Integrate library resources into Blackboard.

Strategy G: Evaluate new Web 2.0 technology/software for usefulness in meeting   other goals. Obtain training/software if it merits use.

Strategy H: Oversee the implementation of a digitization plan for the Library (Digital Initiatives Work Team).

Objective 4: Keep library web content current.

- Implement a content management system (CMS).
- Have the Steely Web Committee serve as a conduit for official, general web content such as "Library News."
- Have the web committee create a matrix of content ownership in order that web content can be edited and maintained by those who create the content.
- Provide training for faculty and staff to edit web content.
- Create guidelines that include timelines for submitting official content, such as news items, to the web committee.
- Create guidelines which suggest a timeline for departments to read and revise departmental web content.

Strategy A: Investigate the implementation of an institutional repository (DIWT).

Objective 5: Ensure that the privacy of critical user and internal data is not compromised.

Development

Goal 1: Expand Steely Library's "margin for excellence" by increasing the level of private giving and increasing the level of grant-funded support.

Objective 1: Complete the fundraising for the Archives Project, Phase II.

Strategy A: Begin formal planning process in cooperation with NKU Architecture Dept.

Strategy B: Build comprehensive effort combining grant-seeking, philanthropy, and potential government support.

Objective 2: Increase number of first time major donors.

Strategy A: Creatively use non-traditional electronic tools to prospect for donors currently not on the University's radar.

Strategy B: Look for opportunities to approach NKU alumni who have moved out of the immediate region.

Objective 3: Increase level of giving by current donors.

Strategy A: Increase the number of FOSL Life members by 10 per year.

Strategy B: Increase the number of FOSL members at all other levels by 25%

      Strategy C: Increase the number and size of donors to the Library Services Account

         i.   Develop and complete spring mailing.
        ii.   Use spring mailing to identify potential major donors for cultivation.

Objective 4: Increase the number of grant applications.

      Strategy A: Through mentorship and encouragement, increase faculty involvement in grant writing process to better leverage the time of Grants Officer.

      Strategy B: Encourage faculty to actively seek out partnerships with both internal and external entities.

      Strategy C: Explore resources available on campus through Research, Grants, & Contracts.

Marketing

Goal 1: Build a marketing orientation within the Library, leading to better communication of library services, creating heightened perceptions of value among the University's internal and external constituencies.

      Objective 1: Marketing Work Team will create a formal marketing/communication plan.
      The following documents were completed summer 2009: Strategic Marketing Communication Plan Draft, Executive Summary, and Timeline. Will be presented to Library September 2009.

         Strategy A: Consult with campus experts such as Marketing professors and Marketing & Communications Department staff.
- MKT 492 Advanced Marketing Research class has conducted Faculty and Student Focus groups. Presented team with Qualitative Research findings from the focus groups.

         Strategy B: Investigate consulting with NKU's Marketing Research Partnering Program.

         Strategy C: Redesign the liaison program in context of marketing efforts. (Liaison program is addressed in Strategic Marketing Communication Plan).

Goal 2: Build an internal marketing orientation within the Library, leading to better communication of library services, events, and projects between Library employees (In Strategic Marketing Communication Plan).

Objective 1: Improve interdepartmental communications.

    Strategy A: Complete the Steely Showcase sessions during FY 2010 by offering sessions in Administration, Access Services and Systems.

    Strategy B: Create a more effective central repository for internal Library information (e.g., blogs, Intranet, directory structure).
- Keep records management in mind, what will be the record copy and who will be responsible for maintaining it?
- Investigate wiki technology as a means of updating library manuals

    Strategy C: Encourage redundant channels of communication.

Goal 3: Work to make Steely Library an example of excellence in terms of "Library as Place."

    Objective 1: Continue to remodel and renovate to make the building more flexible in meeting the needs of today and tomorrow.

    Strategy A: Complete the reconfiguration of the third floor.

    Strategy B: Continue to develop the Loggia as a comfortable place for group gathering and as a flexible space for Library events.

    Strategy C: Continue to identify spaces for renovation needs as funding permits.

    Objective 2: Improve navigation throughout the building.

    Strategy A: Review and revise signage and maps to enable users to more effectively use building resources.

    Objective 3: Make the Steely Library environment more intellectually stimulating and enjoyable through special events.

    Strategy A: Bring performers to the Loggia for live performances.

Faculty Development

Goal: Develop a faculty body that is well prepared to meet the challenges of 21st century librarianship and is engaged in the profession and the community.

    Objective 1: Provide an environment that supports the faculty's engagement in the profession and the community.

Objective 2: Improve hiring process to ensure that new faculty has the skills and abilities needed to function as faculty and are fully aware of the expectations of the University regarding faculty responsibilities.

> **Strategy A:** Ensure that the matter of faculty expectations and responsibilities is adequately addressed in position advertisements and at various points in the interview process: 1) in a session with the RPT Committee; 2) within the supervisor interview; and 3) within the Associate Provost's interview.

Objective 3: Build an effective mentoring program to encourage the development of junior faculty as they progress through the tenure process.

Staff Development

Goal 1: Enhance staff skills to better meet the needs of a 21st century library.

> **Objective 1:** Build staff awareness of best practices at other institutions and throughout the field.

> > **Strategy A.** Continue to develop the Library Staff Blackboard site as a repository for information related to best practices, staff development opportunities, etc.

> **Objective 2:** Investigate ways in which staff from units throughout the Library can participate in an internal professional development program to become aware of programming in areas of the Library beyond their primary assignment.

> > **Strategy A:** Encourage supervisors to foster staff cross-training as appropriate

> > **Strategy B:** Evaluate strategies for creating social opportunities for the employees of Steely Library, encouraging involvement from all constituencies.
> > > i. Establish a monthly informal coffee meeting for faculty and staff members.
> > > ii. Establish a quarterly reception to welcome new Library faculty and staff members.
> > > iii. Establish other avenues such as a newsletter, employee recognition, and social gatherings (picnic)

With suggested updates as of 9/3/09

Last revised October 2008

166 - Documents - (10+ Pages)

Brookens Library's Strategic Plan June 2006

University *of* Illinois *at* Springfield

University of Illinois at Springfield

Table of Contents

Introduction

Executive Summary

168 - Documents - (10+ Pages)

Introduction

The development of this strategic plan for Brookens Library coincides with the 30th anniversary of the Brookens Library building—the building was dedicated on May 19, 1976. The last quarter of the 20th century brought an unprecedented amount of change in libraries as we saw card catalogs first "freeze" and then disappear, computers become ubiquitous, and the internet become the gateway to information. During the same period of time, state funding for higher education began to erode even as inflation in the prices of library resources (many of them now in digital format) continued unabated.

Library policies and practices have not kept up with the rapid technological change or with the change in budgetary realities. In addition, librarians have generally been unprepared for changes in user behavior, in particular the degree to which college students have embraced the web and the various digital tools that are now available to them.

The timing of this strategic planning process, then, could not have been better. It provided an opportunity for the library to re-imagine its future as it enters its next thirty years. The central themes of this plan are people working together creatively and using technology ingeniously to provide excellent library resources and services to the UIS community. A question hangs in the air—does the building still matter? The answer is an emphatic "yes." The library is the campus building that best embodies the spirit of learning, discovery and reflection that define a liberal arts education.

As the UIS strategic plan was bold to state as its strategic intent that it would be one of the best small public liberal arts universities in the nation, so we in the Brookens Library say that we intend to be the exceptional library that defines a great public liberal arts university—an environment that inspires learning and serves as the heart of the campus intellectual community.

Jane Treadwell
University Librarian and Dean of Library Instructional Services
April 28, 2006

Brookens Library Strategic Plan: Executive Summary

1)   Purpose

Mission Statement
At the heart of the intellectually rich, collaborative, and intimate learning environment of UIS, Brookens Library selects, organizes, preserves, and provides access to and instruction in the use of information resources for research, discovery, and lifelong learning.

Vision Statement
Working together creatively and using technology ingeniously, we provide excellent information resources and services to the UIS community.

Guiding Values

Brookens Library strives for excellence in all of our endeavors. We value:

- **Communication** that is open, creative, consultative, and responsive to individual differences and to user and organizational needs;
- **Flexibility** in our services and in the use of our resources to provide for functionality and innovation;
- Creating an **environment of discovery** that facilitates learning and that meets the patrons where they are;
- **Patron-centered service** that assures a positive and unified atmosphere; and
- **Accessibility** by making our diverse services user-friendly.

2)   Strategy for the Future

Statement of Strategic Intent

Brookens Library will be the exceptional library that defines a great public liberal arts university—an environment that inspires learning and serves as the heart of the campus intellectual community.

Environmental Assessment

These environmental factors present challenges and opportunities for Brookens Library:

1. **Enrollment growth and new general education curriculum** will create increased demand for library materials and services as demand from existing customer groups continues unabated.

2. **Online learning**—the growing number of students enrolled in online programs and courses places unique demands on the library.

4

3. **Information technology**—the library must adapt its services to patrons for whom the internet is the first stop in seeking information.

4. **Physical space**—the current library space does not meet the expectations of users and does not provide adequate space for collections.

5. **Budget**—Pressures of inflation in the cost of library materials, salaries for skilled knowledge workers, and renovations to the physical space require additional funding at a time when state funding for higher education is static or declining.

Competitive/Benchmark Analysis

The Brookens Library exceeds the libraries of IBHE and COPLAC peers on most measures captured by the ACRL (Association of College and Research Libraries) statistics. Only two out of eight peer libraries had greater volume counts, and only three had greater total library expenditures. Significantly, the peers that exceeded UIS on these measures also reported library renovations and/or expansions in the past ten-fifteen years.

Compared to the libraries of the private liberal arts colleges selected for benchmarking in the UIS strategic plan, the UIS library held over 100,000 more volumes than the nearest competitor and also had a larger total budget than the other libraries. Again, the libraries closest to UIS in total volumes and library expenditures had undergone renovation and expansion in the past five-fifteen years.

Key Strategic Issue

The overriding strategic issue facing the Brookens Library is how, with limited financial resources, to provide excellent library resources and services to the growing student population that includes undergraduate and graduate students who may live on campus, commute, or receive their UIS education online.

Strategic Goals

1. *Excellence in Information Resources through Superior Access*
- Brookens Library will adjust, adapt, and expand its collection in alignment with the priorities of UIS.
- The Library will put into place technological solutions to help our users locate and retrieve information quickly and efficiently.
- The Library will demonstrate its commitment to partnerships that enhance the services it can provide.
- The library will pursue alternative funding sources for critical initiatives and maximize the impact of its spending through cooperative purchases that lower costs.

5

2. *Services that Anticipate and Respond to User Needs, Preferences, and Trends in Higher Education*
- Discern real user needs and respond to them in a timely and efficient manner.
- Design services that anticipate user needs and preferences.
- Monitor trends in higher education and scholarly publishing for innovative practices the Library should adopt.
- Promote Library services through a vigorous, active, and ongoing marketing campaign.
- Enhance outreach to the local and regional community.

3. *Active Participation in Curriculum Development and Instruction*
- Create an academically successful and information-literate student body.
- Expand reference/point-of-need services.

4. *Physical and Virtual Spaces That Are Open, Inviting and Inspiring*
- Improve physical spaces.
- Improve virtual spaces.

5. *Faculty and Staff Members Who Are Innovative, Collaborative, and Exceptionally Customer Service Oriented*
- Develop a program of customer-service training for new and current library employees.
- Continually review library policies and processes to test for alignment with mission and strategic intent.
- Increase support for faculty and staff professional development.
- Encourage staff to develop innovative and cost-effective solutions.
- Continue to actively pursue collaborative relationships.

6. *Communication that Facilitates Service, Access, Learning, and Assessment*
- Develop and support an effective internal communication system.
- Promote the centrality of the library to the mission of the campus

Stretch Ideas
1. Integrate access tools to support patron research with goal of one search box access to resources.
2. Find ways to fulfill all resource needs for our distance learners.
3. Assign a personal library advisor to each UIS student.
4. Offer librarian office hours in academic departments, student commons areas, and other areas outside of the library building.
5. Merge Access Services and Reference service points.
6. Investigate the possibility of a minor in Information Studies.
7. Create an internet café on Level One of the building.
8. Seek funding for the renovation of Brookens Library.

6

3) Resources Plan for Achieving Strategic Goals

Resources Needed

We estimate that $14,682,000 will be required in one-time costs, of which $14,000,000 is the current estimate for a total renovation of Brookens Library. Recurring costs associated with this plan total $392,967 representing costs for new staff, inflation in the prices of library resources, equipment replacement, and software licenses.

Resource Procurement Strategy

The Library plans to seek grants and other private funding for many of the start-up and other one-time costs associated with this plan; however, recurring funding will be required to insure the long-term viability of new library services. In general, UIS needs to protect the investment that it has already made in building an exceptional library and extend that commitment into the future. Partnerships with the other two University of Illinois libraries allow the Brookens Library to enhance the number and quality of electronic resources that we provide to the UIS community. These partnerships and other consortial relationships must be sustained.

4) Monitoring and Evaluation

Performance results are included under each thrust as part of the Strategic Goals statements in Section 2.

7

Section 1: Purpose

Mission Statement

At the heart of the intellectually rich, collaborative, and intimate learning environment of UIS, Brookens Library selects, organizes, preserves, and provides access to and instruction in the use of information resources for research, discovery, and lifelong learning.

Vision Statement

Working together creatively and using technology ingeniously, we provide excellent information resources and services to the UIS community.

Guiding Values

Brookens Library strives for excellence in all of our endeavors. We value:
- **Communication** that is open, creative, consultative, and responsive to individual differences and to user and organizational needs;
- **Flexibility** in our services and in the use of our resources to provide for functionality and innovation;
- Creating an **environment of discovery** that facilitates learning and that meets the patrons where they are;
- **Patron-centered service** that assures a positive and unified atmosphere; and
- **Accessibility** by making our diverse services user-friendly.

Mandates Impacting Brookens Library

--University of Illinois mandates

--University of Illinois at Springfield mandates and policies

--federal copyright law

--USA Patriot Act

Mandates specifically pertaining to libraries:

-Library Records Confidentiality Act

-Protection of Library Materials Act

-Library Bill of Rights (American Library Association)

- Freedom to Read Statement (American Library Association)

These mandates are reflected in Brookens Library partnerships and policies, such as:

174 - Documents - (10+ Pages)

-membership in the ILLINET network of the Online Computer Library Center (OCLC), an international bibliographic utility, to which we contribute original bibliographic records and holdings data for shared resource distribution;

-membership in Consortium of Academic and Research Libraries in Illinois (CARLI), a statewide administrative agency which leads Illinois academic libraries to create and sustain a rich, supportive, and diverse knowledge environment that furthers teaching, learning, and research through the sharing of collections, expertise and programs;

-membership in the Rolling Prairie Library System (RPLS), which requires participation in interlibrary loan functions and other resource sharing activities;

-partnerships with our sister campus libraries for purchases, licensing of, and access to, electronic databases across the entire U of I System;

-Library policies concerning the acquisition, cataloging and classification, circulation and access, preservation, withdrawal, and donation of library materials; and

-policies on copyright and fair use.

Section 2: Strategy for the Future

Statement of Strategic Intent

Brookens Library will be the exceptional library that defines a great public liberal arts university—an environment that inspires learning and serves as the heart of the campus intellectual community

Environmental Assessment

For UIS Brookens Library, these environmental factors present challenges and opportunities:
1. Enrollment growth and new general education curriculum
2. Online Learning
3. Information Technology
4. Physical space
5. Budget

Enrollment growth and new general education curriculum
UIS begins to admit an expanded freshman class in the Fall 2006 that will increase the campus FTE each year. Accompanying the growth in the student body is a new general education curriculum that will be implemented in the Fall 2006. Both of these factors will create increased demand for library materials and services that will require the library to purchase materials and build collections in new areas, while the need to support existing academic programs continues. The campus growth in first and second year students will also increase demand for library user education delivered by instructional services librarians. At the same time, demand from transfer and graduate students will remain steady.

Online Learning
Approximately forty percent of UIS students are enrolled in online learning courses or programs. The library is an essential resource for online learners, and specific emphasis must be directed at improving the tools Brookens uses to deliver both print and online content to this population regardless of their location.

Information Technology
Students, faculty, staff and lifelong learners have changed their information seeking behaviors and now begin research using electronic, rather than print, information via the internet. Expertise in staying current with, adopting, and implementing technologies that integrate new software, hardware, and deliver e-information to users has become a critical function of the library. A stronger partnership with campus Information Technology Services and OTEL, as well as the development of library staff with technology skills will be important to create the technical infrastructure that supports new methods of academic inquiry.

Physical Space
Students and faculty have expressed a need for more aesthetically pleasing and flexible spaces equipped with technology to support collaborative teaching and learning. The current library

space is not configured to maximize access to computers, collections, group space or classrooms, or to encourage spending time in the Library Reports from 2003 and 2005 document problems with the building and offer potential solutions. Comparable universities have invested significant resources to renovate and reconfigure libraries to reflect changing university community needs.

Budget

Planned growth within the university of students and faculty, and a new curriculum will necessitate growth in the library. Support for additional hiring, collections, services, and space is not adequate at current state funding levels. The pressures of inflation in library materials, salaries for skilled knowledgeable workers, and renovations to physical space can only be accomplished through development of adequate budgets.

Competitive/Benchmark Analysis

The Library used two groups for comparison: COPLAC/IBHE peers and the set of private liberal arts colleges in Illinois that had been used for benchmarking in the UIS Strategic Plan. COPLAC (Council of Public Liberal Arts Colleges) is an aspirational peer group for UIS. The Illinois Board of Higher Education (IBHE) has also assigned a set of peer institutions for UIS.

COPLAC/IBHE Peers

College and university libraries report statistics on a national basis to two organizations: the Association of College and Research Libraries (ACRL), which publishes statistics annually, and the National Center for Education Statistics, which publishes its Academic Library Statistics (ALS) biannually. For these comparisons, we used the ACRL Statistics for 2004; although ALS was collected in 2004, it hasn't published statistics since 2002.

For this comparison, members of either the COPLAC or IBHE peer groups that submitted data to ACRL in 2004 were chosen. Since submission to ACRL is voluntary, many of the peer institutions identified by IBHE or as members of COPLAC did not submit data and therefore are not present in the published statistics. The comparison set consists of COPLAC and IBHE peer group members that submitted data to ACRL and that were identified as Carnegie "Master's/Professional" classification, along with one Doctoral institution (University of South Dakota) on the IBHE list. This yielded nine peer institutions with data in the 2004 ACRL.

On almost every measure reported by ACRL (see Appendix B for definitions), Brookens Library exceeds our peer institution libraries. Only two elite private liberal arts universities, Trinity University and Union College, and the one doctoral institution, the University of South Dakota, have higher volume counts than Brookens Library. Trinity, Truman State, and Union College all show larger total library expenditures than UIS, but only two institutions, Trinity and Union College, spend more on library materials. A major difference between Brookens Library and these other libraries is the status of the library building. The libraries at both Trinity University and Union College have undergone major expansion and/or renovation during the past few years and the library at Truman State was expanded and renovated in 1993. (Information on peer library facilities was obtained from library web pages.)

11

University of Illinois at Springfield

Private Liberal Arts Colleges in Illinois

We also looked at Brookens Library in comparison to the private liberal arts colleges in Illinois that UIS used for benchmarking in the campus strategic plan. Here the results were even more striking. On nearly every measure reported to ACRL, Brookens exceeds the figures reported by this set of Illinois liberal arts colleges. For instance, Brookens holds 536,743 total volumes while the nearest competitor, Bradley University, holds 435,366. In this instance, however, several of the institutions are in the "Bachelor's degree" category rather than the "Master's/Professional" category to which UIS belongs.

Again, a major difference between these other libraries and Brookens Library at UIS has to do with the library facilities. (Information about facilities of this peer group was obtained from library web pages and telephone and/or e-mail conversations with library directors at these institutions.) Bradley, at 107,000 square feet, and Illinois Wesleyan, at 103,000, each has much greater room for collections and student seating than UIS. With over 100,000 more volumes than these two peers, the Brookens Library (including the parts devoted to ITS Media Services) only has 89,000 square feet devoted to the library. Illinois Wesleyan moved into a new library building, the Ames Library, in 2003. Both Bradley University and Knox College had major library renovations and/or expansions in the early 1990's. McKendree College is in the planning stages for a major expansion, having raised funds for this purpose in a recent capital campaign. Knox College proudly proclaims that its Seymour Library, "recently ranked 15th in the country by the 2002 *Princeton Review,* is a student's dream…"

These data suggest that Brookens Library could be a major selling point to potential new students and faculty if the library facility lived up to the collections and other measures of library quality.

12

Strengths, Weaknesses, Opportunities, and Threats (SWOT) Analysis

Brookens Library Strengths:
- Dedicated, creative library personnel
- Statewide and national library alliances and partnerships (CARLI, I-Share, OCLC)*--Brookens Library is fortunate to be located in a state with a strong tradition of library cooperation and resource sharing
- Knowledge and use of current technologies to support learning and research
- Accessibility of collections and services, both on-campus and online
- Size of Brookens collection compared to peers
- Library administration interested in staff development/administrative support

Brookens Library Weaknesses
- Inadequate state funding
- A building which is outdated and a library footprint that is too small for current collections and services
- Lack of dedicated IT support
- Staff issues (salary issues, wearing too many hats, hierarchy among staff)

Brookens Library Opportunities
- Collaborations and partnerships with UIS programs and departments, the other two University of Illinois campuses, and state and national library consortia to provide top-of-the-line services and resources
- Partner with OTEL (Office of Technology Enhanced Learning) and the colleges to provide expanded library services and resources to online students, including embedding library modules into course management systems
- Changing UIS campus: general education will lead to more opportunities for teaching and information literacy initiatives
- Increased fundraising opportunities

Brookens Library Threats/Challenges
- Reduced or stagnant state funding leading to decreased availability of resources
- Online competition by for-profit and free information providers
- Possibility of losing more Brookens space
- Uncertainty about where the library falls in the list of campus priorities
- Changing UIS campus: general education will require the library to purchase materials and provide services in new areas, while still supporting existing programs at the undergraduate and graduate levels

*CARLI—Consortium of Academic and Research Libraries in Illinois
I-Share—the 65 CARLI libraries that share an online catalog
OCLC—Online Computer Library Center, the world's largest library cooperative

University of Illinois at Springfield

Key Strategic Issues Facing the Organization

The overriding strategic issue facing the Brookens Library is how, with limited financial resources, to provide excellent library resources and services to the growing student population that includes undergraduate and graduate students who may live on campus, commute, or receive their UIS education online.

Three other questions follow from the first:

- How to provide excellent support for a curriculum that is changing to reflect the UIS aspiration to become one of the nation's top five small public liberal arts universities?

- How to fulfill the need for library instruction generated by the greater numbers of undergraduate students with little, if any, experience in using a university library?

- How to transform the library's physical and virtual spaces into the attractive, flexible and collaborative learning environment desired and expected at a great liberal arts university?

Other important strategic issues include:

- How to respond to the changing learning styles and technology preferences of college students?

- In an increasingly "Googleized" world, how can the library more effectively demonstrate the value of our collections and services?

- Where do we focus our energies—on teaching how to use the library or on making the library (especially the virtual library) easier to use? Can we pursue both strategies simultaneously?

- How do we secure funding for the major needs that this plan identifies?

- How can we allocate limited staff resources and improve internal communication to maximize our effectiveness as an organization?

14

180 - Documents - (10+ Pages)

Strategic Goals and Thrusts

Goal #1

EXCELLENCE IN INFORMATION RESOURCES THROUGH SUPERIOR ACCESS

Thrust #1: Excellence in the UIS library collection
The cornerstone of an academic library is the collection that is built for its specific user communities. Brookens Library will adjust, adapt, and expand its collection in alignment with the priorities at UIS.

Action Steps:
- Develop and manage a locally-housed collection to support current curriculum, research, and lifelong learning.
- Develop and manage a virtual collection that includes purchased and freely-available content to support the academic community.
- Design and implement a collection assessment program.
- Increase access to online sources available from the Urbana and Chicago campus libraries.
- Maintain strong communication with library users to stay abreast of their information needs.

Performance Indicators:
1. Increase in usage of collections
2. Match local purchases to standard collection lists
3. Most required readings available at time of course start-up
4. Fewer faculty trips to UIUC and UIC to conduct research
5. Library faculty membership on all UIS curriculum committees

Thrust #2: Implement tools to enhance user access to all library resources
Faced with an overwhelming array of information sources and options, patrons rely on the library to present organized and guided approaches for information discovery. We will use current technologies and will search for more advanced technological solutions to enhance the user's ability to locate and retrieve information quickly and efficiently.
Action Steps:

- Adopt improved methods of document delivery; increase choices for patrons to select delivery methods.
- Restructure website as a portal to research.
- Increase presence of Library information in course management system pages.
- Improve authority control and description.
- Integrate access tools to support patron research with goal of one search box access to resources.*
- Participate in experiments with multiple electronic platforms to surface library content on the open web.
- Implement new digital library products.
- Find ways to fulfill resource needs for our distance learners.*

15

University of Illinois at Springfield

Performance indicators:
1. Demonstrate increased usage through statistics from library website and vendors reports
2. Increase in number of course management pages with Library content
3. Distance users report increased satisfaction with resources available to them
4. Performance testing of access to resources by measuring factors such as response time, down time and user logins to web sites.
5. Survey UIS community about satisfaction with access to information resources both before and after projects' completion
6. Track projects started and completed based on these action items

Thrust #3: Excellence in Collaboration
The success of an individual library is dependent upon building and sustaining relationships with its patrons, other libraries, library consortia, and the publishers and vendors in the marketplace. Brookens Library will demonstrate its commitment to partnerships that enhance the services it can provide.

Action Steps:
- Explore new partnerships while expanding and solidifying regional, national and international partnerships to improve access to resources.
- Increase use of services and products provided by library vendors to streamline and to enhance local processes.

Performance Indicators:
1. Growth in the quantity and quality of access to services and collections
2. Documented improvement in local workflow to select, order, acquire, and catalog materials

Thrust #4: Excellence in leveraging the budget to fulfill goals
State budget support has failed to keep pace with the rate of increase in library expenditures. The library will pursue alternative funding sources for critical initiatives and maximize the impact of its spending through cooperative purchases that lower costs.

Action Steps:
- Identify grant sources to fund collection projects.
- Cultivate donors for gifts to expand collections.
- Create guiding principles for the collection budget.
- Develop shared storage policy among University of Illinois libraries.
- Increase participation in shared licenses that reduce the cost of electronic resources.

Performance indicators:
1. Increase in grant money awarded
2. Increase in number of gifts/donations received
3. Collection development policy
4. Increased number of shared licenses

* = Stretch Idea

16

Goal #2

SERVICES THAT ANTICIPATE AND RESPOND TO USER NEEDS, PREFERENCES, AND TRENDS IN HIGHER EDUCATION

Thrust #1: Discern real user needs and respond to them in a timely and efficient manner
Library users can be local or online and increasingly operate in a 24 X 7 digital world. The library will solicit their input on the need to create or redesign services to support inquiry and learning regardless of location.

Action Steps:
- Implement an online feedback form to continually receive input from students, faculty, staff, and other library users.
- Conduct periodic user surveys and focus groups and act on results.
- Analyze data collected internally or supplied by vendors or other appropriate agencies.
- Create a mechanism to continually incorporate feedback from users into decision-making processes, policies and procedures.
- Participate in the LibQual survey of service quality to assess our performance.

Performance Indicators:
1) Prepare an annual report on how user feedback and other data were used to make changes and improvements.
2) Analyze LibQual and other survey results to improve library services.

Thrust #2: Design services that anticipate user needs and preferences
The demographics of UIS students, faculty and staff suggest a wide variation in experience in the use of a library and computing skills for academic work. The library will draw on successful models to personalize services that assist users at their level of ability.

Action Steps:
- Seek out best practices and innovative ideas from academic libraries.
- Assign a personal Library advisor to each UIS student (start with pilot program).*
- Leverage collaborative relationships to bring new services to Brookens Library.
- Capitalize on the personal devices and ways of sharing information that are preferred by many younger students.

Performance Indicators:
1) Evaluate student perception of usefulness of Library advisor
2) Survey faculty perception on student improvement with Library advisor
3) Assess services against peer group benchmarks
4) Document student use of personal devices to access library information

Thrust #3: Continually monitor trends in higher education and scholarly publishing for innovative practices that the Library should adopt
Libraries and universities face a real and growing gap between the rising costs of publishing and declining budgets that erode purchasing power. However, the responsibility to provide access to

an increasing body of research remains. National and international efforts underway to provide innovative solutions to collect and preserve academic research and content will inform UIS strategies.

Action Steps:
- Establish and maintain an institutional repository for publications of the UIS scholarly community.
- Adopt a standard of digital theses submission and archiving processes.
- Participate in development of University of Illinois-wide action plan to address issues in scholarly communication.
- Coordinate implementation of the U of I scholarly communication plan at UIS.

Performance Indicators:
1) Annual count of publications submitted to the institutional respository
2) Comparison of numbers of graduating Master's degree students versus number of digital thesis submissions

Thrust #4: Promote Library services through a vigorous, active and ongoing marketing campaign
Brookens Library will initiate a campaign both to educate the UIS community about the array of services and collections available to them and also to increase participation in library-designed events.

Action Steps:
- Develop a marketing plan that includes Brookens Library "brand".
- Utilize campus print, electronic media, and local and regional newspapers on a regular basis.
- Use appropriate promotional techniques to target specific markets within our community.

Performance Indicators:
1) Increased event attendance
2) Increased gate counts
3) Increased hits on web pages
4) Increased usage of databases
5) Offers of opportunities to partner with or create services for campus or community initiatives

Thrust #5: Enhance outreach to the local and regional community
Specialized resources, collections, and services that are of particular benefit to the community users of Brookens Library will be highlighted via news sources and publications most likely to reach the wider public audience. At the same time, the community will be cultivated to provide support for Brookens Library.

Action Steps:
- Increase services of and advertising for the Central Illinois Nonprofit Resource Center.
- Increase visibility of Illinois Regional Archives Depository.

- Develop plan with Friends of Brookens Library board to become a partner in Library fundraising.

Performance Indicators:
1) Measurable growth in use of services and collections
2) Increased donations/gifts due to the Friends of Brookens Library board fundraising

*=Stretch idea

Goal #3

ACTIVE PARTICIPATION IN CURRICULUM DEVELOPMENT AND INSTRUCTION

Thrust #1: Create an academically successful and information-literate student body.
Information literacy is one of the goals of the new UIS general education curriculum. Information literacy skills are to be implemented in various courses, but, like writing, information literacy skills will not be maintained unless they are reinforced throughout a student's university career. Promoting "information literacy across the curriculum" will create UIS graduates who are skilled at finding, evaluating, and using information in their careers and in their daily lives.

Action Steps:
- Engage expert consultant for needs assessment.
- Increase individual consultations for specific courses.
- Conduct faculty development workshops on incorporating information literacy into the curriculum.
- Strengthen relationships with faculty to build cooperation for information literacy efforts.
- Develop and offer a series of workshops on specific library topics (for example, Bibliographic Software, Master's Thesis Research, workshops on various online resources).
- Lobby for a required unit on Library Research in all General Education composition classes.
- Develop a research course as a General Education elective.
- Investigate the possibility of a minor in Information Studies.*

Performance Indicators:
1) Increased campus-wide faculty participation in library-sponsored faculty development programs
2) Increased number of course-integrated research sessions and increased presence of library instruction modules in the BlackBoards for particular courses
3) Improved performance by students, as reported by instructors or gleaned through librarian-instructor collaboration in grading
4) Favorable evaluations of workshops

Thrust #2: Expand reference/point-of-need services

19

University of Illinois at Springfield

Because of changing on-campus demographics and the increase in online students, we will be flexible in our reference services, offering more services in different venues, and through different media. We will also offer more workshops for the entire campus.

Action Steps:
- Offer librarian office hours in academic departments, student commons areas, and other areas.*
- Increase virtual reference.
- Develop interactive instructional modules.
- Increase presence of information about library resources and services in course management system pages.
- Establish library/research advisors.*
- Provide special assistance to faculty in the use of online resources.

Performance Indicators:
1) Statistics on the number and nature of reference transactions should increase as these new programs are implemented
2) Improved performance by students, as reported by instructors
3) Increased understanding of and satisfaction with Library services as measured by surveys, etc.
4) Increased number of course management system pages with Library content

* = Stretch idea

Goal #4

PHYSICAL AND VIRTUAL SPACES THAT ARE OPEN, INVITING, AND INSPIRING

Brookens Library strives to provide a learning environment in which new and future library services can be imagined and developed in partnership with the campus community. These learning spaces need to be physical as well as virtual.

Thrust #1: Improve physical spaces
A space needs assessment of Brookens Library in 2003 found that the facility as it currently exists limits the ability of the library to "function, serve and grow." However, the study also noted that "this large, flexible building can be reshaped into a powerful center for learning, teaching and research." A conceptual plan for a renovated Brookens developed in 2005 affirmed this concept with one possible design that emphasized attractive, flexible spaces for users.

Action steps:

Short term:
- Merger of access services and reference service points.*
- Continued development of lounges, learning commons and group study spaces

20

- Improved, up-to-date, effective signage.
- Internet Café on Level I.*
- Replace worn furniture with attractive, inviting, comfortable and efficient furniture.
- Art pieces in selected areas.

Longer term:
- Define program for Brookens renovation, using data from 2003 report and concepts from 2005 report.*
- Seek funding for renovation.*

Performance Indicators:
1) Higher gate count and circulation statistics
2) Increased user satisfaction as measured by surveys, etc.
3) Library is included in UIS promotional literature

Thrust #2: Improve virtual spaces
Many of today's college students have grown up with and feel comfortable in, a virtual or online environment. In the library, these virtual spaces comprise the interface between library users and staff and the growing world of information available online and in electronic sources. Access to these virtual spaces requires up-to-date computer hardware and software, networked and wireless internet access, an attractive and easily navigated library web site, and access to portable and hand-held electronic devices.

- Enhance Library web pages with attractive interface and design, transparent and intuitive navigation, RSS and CSS feeds.
- Increase the number of computer work stations throughout the Library.
- Create a digital repository.
- Improve wireless access throughout building.
- Include popular new technologies in Library lending policies.
- Expand availability of audio books and podcasting materials.
- Find and implement a one-search-box portal to all online library resources.*

Performance Indicators:
1) Increased user satisfaction as measured by surveys, etc.
2) More hits on Library web pages
3) Increased user satisfaction with online resources as measured by surveys, etc.
4) Increased borrowing of laptops and iPods

*= Stretch Idea

Goal #5

FACULTY AND STAFF MEMBERS WHO ARE INNOVATIVE, COLLABORATIVE, AND EXCEPTIONALLY CUSTOMER SERVICE ORIENTED

21

University of Illinois at Springfield

Thrust #1: Develop a program of customer-service training for new and current library employees
The library is responsible for providing the tools and training to educate employees to provide excellent customer service. Training will provide a baseline of knowledge and empower Library employees to fulfill the mission of Brookens.

Action Steps:
- Identify and train Library faculty and staff who will serve as in-house customer-service trainers.
- Provide customer-service training for all current and new Library faculty, staff and student assistants.
- Provide refresher training at regular intervals.
- Develop a customer service web tutorial.

Performance indicators:
1) Review customer surveys for evidence of improved service
2) Compare LibQual results with those of peer institutions

Thrust #2: Continually review library policies and processes to test for alignment with mission and strategic intent
While it is critical to maintain a set of policies for the organization, a process of regular review will surface any need to adjust rules and workflow for improvement.

Action Steps:
- Develop and adopt a service mission and keep it posted.
- Seek innovative and efficient processes.
- Seek customer-focused processes.
- Develop new ways to get feedback (Preview Days, etc.).
- Make policies and procedures available on the intranet.
- Push decision-making authority further down in the organizational structure.

Performance indicators:
1) Document how new processes are working
2) Common understanding of policies
3) Fewer customer complaints

Thrust # 3: Increase support for faculty and staff professional development
The cost of keeping faculty and staff current in trends, technologies, and best practices in libraries is an investment in employee satisfaction and retention. Knowledgeable library employees will also improve the quality of library services and teaching for the UIS community.

- Adapt innovative ideas of other institutions to our situation.
- Identify priority areas for development.
- Create staff mentor system.

Performance indicator:
1) New programs and processes as a result of professional development activities

22

Thrust #4: **Encourage staff to develop innovative and cost-effective solutions**
Employees at all levels of an organization discover ways to improve workflow, save money, and offer new services. The library will facilitate an environment that values faculty, staff, and student input.

- Develop mechanisms for staff to easily make suggestions.
- Develop strategies for supervisors to use to encourage staff input.
- Create system of meaningful but inexpensive rewards.

Performance indicator:
1) Document changes and improvements as a result of suggestions

Thrust 5: **Continue to actively pursue collaborative relationships**
To foster dynamic, informed, innovative, and respectful interactions within the library, the campus, the U of Illinois system, and wider library organizations, the library will enable staff to consider new ways of working with colleagues.

- Encourage projects across Library departmental lines.
- Increase cross-training within and across Library departments.
- Strengthen collaborative relationships on campus and with institutions throughout the state, especially the other U of I campuses.
- Seek opportunities for additional collaboration.

Performance indicator:
1) Periodically review collaborative relationships for evidence of benefits

Goal #6

COMMUNICATION THAT FACILITATES SERVICE, ACCESS, LEARNING, AND ASSESSMENT

In order to provide outstanding services to our users (UIS students, faculty, and staff and the Springfield community) and to build a greater sense of community within the library, the employees of Brookens Library will enhance internal communications. All Library employees will recognize the importance of their participation in developing and fulfilling the Library's mission and goals. The Library will also reinforce the Library's centrality to the mission of UIS by better publicizing its services to its core users.

Thrust #1: **An effective internal communication system**
Successful organizational communication will be achieved through both formal and informal means. Opportunities for informal communication help build community and increase comfort levels for discussing issues in meetings and other formal environments. In addition, avenues for formal communication will be increased.

Action Steps:

23

- Implement Brookens Library Intranet so that minutes of meetings, calendars, and project plans will be readily available to all Brookens Library employees.
- All committees and units will share information about projects and other developments in a timely manner at Library Cabinet and staff meetings, and minutes will be published on the Intranet.
- Staff meetings will be scheduled at regular intervals and agendas will include issues of importance to Library employees.
- The Dean will report to the Library about initiatives and activities.
- Create a centralized break/meeting room for all Library employees.
- Develop an effective, structured orientation for new employees.
- Train unit heads in team building techniques to encourage more staff participation in decision-making.
- Create an atmosphere of respect for all library employees.
- Create Library "talking points" and distribute to all employees.

Performance Indicators:
1) Minutes posted on Library Intranet within two weeks of meetings
2) Hits on Intranet increase
3) Suggestions submitted via Intranet will increase
4) Staff meetings occur on a bi-monthly basis
5) New break/meeting room is used regularly by a majority of employees
6) Staff report greater knowledge due to orientation program
7) Employees can speak knowledgeably about important library initiatives

Thrust #2: Promote the centrality of the library to the mission of the campus.
The library is at the heart of all academic endeavors, and Brookens Library will ensure that the campus is aware of its importance to the instructional and scholarly mission of UIS. A strong publicity program will help, as will specific outreach to faculty, staff, and students.

Action Steps:
- Develop coherent avenues for publicizing events.
- Dedicate staff to produce publicity: news releases, posters, invitations, flyers, cards, newsletters, etc..
- Develop a regular library orientation for new faculty (and put back-up information on library web site).
- Send letters to new faculty before the beginning of the academic year with information on collection- and instruction-related resources and services.
- Assign Library/research advisors to incoming students.*
- Develop promotional events for students throughout the year.
- Use the Library web site as one avenue to promote all Library activities and initiatives.

Performance Indicators:
1) Increased attendance at Library-sponsored events
2) Faculty will report better understanding of the Library due to orientation
3) Student attendance at library events will increase
4) Students and faculty will report satisfaction with Library/research advisor program

* = **Stretch Idea**

Stretch Ideas

1. Integrate access tools to support patron research with goal of one search box access to resources.
A 2005 study by OCLC, *Perceptions of Libraries and Information Resources*, found that among college students, 89% begin their search for information by using an Internet search engine such as Google. Only two percent start with the library web site. We believe that it is important for students to be able to find and evaluate information for their scholarly research. The library possesses a treasure trove of scholarly information, but our own search tools often make that information difficult to locate. We need to make the process of searching for library resources much simpler. To that end, we are planning to go outside the box of on the shelf offerings to libraries, to see if we can find and implement a search engine that will truly allow one search of all library resources.

2. Find ways to fulfill all resource needs for our distance learners.
Generally, online users whether in Lincoln Residence Hall or Lincoln, Nebraska, can access all of Brookens Library's online information resources. However, sometimes students are still required to read books for their courses, or to use audio-visual materials. We can send books and other materials to students via interlibrary loan, but sometimes interlibrary loan is too slow, either because the student is far away (Japan, for instance) or the turnaround time is too tight to allow for traditional ILL. We need to begin searching for a systematic way to address these problems. On one front, we should initiate discussions within the local consortium and at the national (OCLC) level concerning expanding the definition of a borrower to include students taking classes at universities some distance away. On another front, we should find ways within copyright guidelines to scan and make print or audiovisual materials available to the distant student for a short window of time. As instructors have been able to recreate the classroom experience for students at a distance, we will seek to recreate the library experience in more depth than is currently possible.

3. Assign a personal library advisor to each UIS student.
Frequently students feel intimidated by the library and especially seem to avoid asking reference questions. We would like to turn things around and take the librarian to them. In much the way that a first-year student is assigned an academic advisor, we propose to assign a library advisor to each student. As the academic advisor helps the student navigate the confusing world of choices concerning courses and a major, the library advisor would help the student with the many choices concerning academic research. Studies have shown that people will turn to a trusted source for information—we plan to make Brookens Library that trusted source. Since the time required for this program is unknown, we would plan to start with a pilot program, most likely involving Capital Scholars.

4. Offer librarian office hours in academic departments, student commons areas, and other areas.
As with the stretch idea above, this idea involves librarians going out to where our campus users are. Librarian office hours in academic departments would make the librarian available to faculty for consultation concerning the collections, particular databases, upcoming instructional sessions, or research needs of their students. By being available in student commons areas, librarians would meet the students on their own turf.

5. Merge Access Services and Reference service points.
Discussions among Access Services and Instructional Services faculty and staff last year concerning a reconfiguration of space on Level 2 yielded the insight that most likely all patron

25

transactions could occur at one desk. Currently, there are a substantial number of referrals from one desk to the other, and students don't appear to mind going to the Circulation Desk whereas there seems to be a certain degree of anxiety involved in approaching the Reference Desk (see stretch idea number 3, above). By offering a "one stop shopping" desk, our users can approach the one desk no matter what their information needs may be.

6. Investigate the possibility of a minor in Information Studies.

Information Studies focuses on the growing importance of information in the global society. A minor in Information Studies would complement majors in various liberal arts and sciences disciplines as well as majors in professional fields. Coursework could include topic such as the economics of information, the politics of information, censorship, and scholarly communication. Because the resource needs for this stretch idea would involve hiring at least two additional library faculty and creating a more traditional academic department within the library, we have not listed this item among our resource needs—we are at the point of investigation only.

7. Create an Internet Café on Level 1.

The idea of a coffee shop on level one of Brookens Library has been around for a long time. Even though another action step of the Library strategic plan is to seek funding for a renovation of the building, we believe that in the short-term we should pursue a café on Level 1. Capitol Perks is a wonderful service to the campus, but the setting in the PAC lobby does not create the cozy intimate feel of a true coffee shop. A café on Level 1 of the library would provide a place for students to read, study and surf the internet in an atmosphere more like that of Barnes & Noble or Starbucks.

8. Seek funding for the renovation of Brookens Library.

It seems odd that renovating a thirty year old library facility and finding enough space for the library collection would be listed as a stretch idea, but in the climate of reduced funding for higher education maintaining and improving the physical infrastructure on a public campus is a daunting task. In our competitive analysis, we found that the only significant element in which the Brookens Library lags behind our peers--even highly-rated private schools--is the library facility. We have also found in student surveys and focus groups that the library building itself is a major impediment to library use. A renovated Brookens Library could become a selling point for UIS as we seek to become one of the best small public liberal arts universities in the nation.

Section 3: Resource Plan for Achieving Strategic Goals

Resources Needed

	One Time	Recurring	SUBTOTAL
Goal #1: Excellence in Information Access & Resource Needs			
◄ Yearly 10% Increase for materials above inflation		$ 93,567	
◄ Library systems specialist		$ 60,000	
† ◄ One search box access to resources	$ 30,000	$ 20,000	
◄ Funding for new products & services			
† -Electronic resource management system (ERM)	$ 15,000	$ 5,000	
† -Table of contents in online book catalog	$ 15,000	$ 5,000	
† -Advanced software for electronic interlibrary loan	$ 15,000	$ 5,000	
	$ 75,000	$ 188,567	$ 263,567
Goal #2: Services that Anticipate/Respond to User Needs & Preferences & Trends in Higher Education			
◄ LibQual participation fees to conduct surveys		$ 2,250	
◄ Full-time marketing/publicity staff position (including fundraising)		$ 30,000	
◄ Marketing and publicity funds		$ 10,000	
◄ Metadata specialist		$ 48,000	
◄ Increased student worker budget		$ 10,000	
† ◄ Scholarly communication education campaign	$ 5,000		
◄ Hire skilled assistants to help with technical questions		$ 10,000	
◄ GA for Nonprofit Resource Center		$ 7,425	
	$ 5,000	$ 117,675	$ 122,675
Goal #3: Active participation in Curriculum Development & Instruction			
† ◄ Faculty development for information literacy-$25,000 grant for 3 yrs	$ 75,000		
◄ GA or paid internship for information literacy		$ 7,425	
◄ Electronic classroom for 25	$ 50,000		
	$ 125,000	$ 7,425	$ 132,425
Goal #4: Physical & Virtual Spaces that Are Open, Inviting & Inspiring			
(Short-Term)			
◄ Planning/programming	$ 200,000		
◄ SGA request for reupholstering existing chairs	$ 12,000		
◄ Updated signage	$ 100,000		
◄ Café construction; outsource operation to Food Service	$ 50,000		
◄ Development of new user spaces	$ 100,000		
◄ Annual computer equipment replacement (4 yr. rotation) & services		$ 27,300	
	$ 462,000	$ 27,300	$ 489,300
(Long-Term)			
† ◄ Library renovation	$14,000,000		$14,000,000
Goal #5: Faculty and Staff Members Who Are Innovative, Collaborative, and Exceptionally Customer Service Oriented			
† ◄ Funds for customer-service training consultant	$ 10,000		
◄ Increase professional development funds		$ 17,000	$ 27,000
Goal #6: Communication			
◄ Web specialist		$ 35,000	
† ◄ Funds to remodel a staff break room	$ 5,000		$ 40,000
GRAND TOTAL	$14,682,000	$392,967	$15,074,967

† We will seek grants and other outside funding for these items.

Total new FTE needed: 4 staff, 2 graduate assistants, and 3 student assistants at 20 hours per week.

University of Illinois at Springfield

Resources Procurement Strategy

The resource plan for achieving Brookens Library's strategic goals recognizes the realities of state funding and, apart from the goal of renovating the Library, would require an investment of just a little over $1 million. We plan to seek grants or other private funding for many of the start-up funds associated with this plan, as designated on the resource plan list. However, recurring funding will be required to operationalize these new library services.

In general, UIS needs to protect the investment that it has already made in building an exceptional library and to extend that commitment to excellence in collections, services, and the library facility into the future. The new general education curriculum, the robust online program, the increase in the number of students, and the university's desire to be among the top five small public liberal arts universities all demand that the library achieve a strong level of funding.

Partnerships with the libraries at the University of Illinois at Urbana-Champaign and the University of Illinois at Chicago allow Brookens Library to purchase resources that otherwise would have been completely out of reach, but these partnerships are not without costs. Although as a percentage of the total the UIS share of any joint purchase is very small, the amounts that Brookens pays to participate along with two large research libraries is still substantial by medium-sized library standards. These U of I resources make for real competitive advantages, however, and need to be sustained.

Similarly, it is crucial that we make the investment in technologies to facilitate our services as detailed throughout the plan. UIS is earning recognition for its online programs and the wireless campus. Using technology to provide sophisticated solutions for our customers has become a UIS way of life, and the Library needs to be much more aggressive in implementing technology to improve services. Several new positions (Systems specialist, metadata specialist, and web specialist) also relate to this need to make better use of technology in pursuing our goals.

Finally, resources are especially needed to make the library facility signal to the world that a great library is behind its doors.

Section 4: Monitoring/Evaluation of Plan Implementation and Results

Timetable

The majority of action steps included in this plan can be started on right away with tangible results expected in two to three years. A few of the items can be started and finished within a year. We have indicated that the goal of securing the funding for a total renovation of the library building is a long-term goal that may not be achieved during the five year timeframe of this strategic plan.

We recognize that in order to implement this plan an additional project management layer will need to be applied to each of the thrusts and action steps. Instead of creating a separate team to implement the Strategic Plan, the Dean's Cabinet, consisting of the Dean and the unit heads within the Library, will be responsible for implementing, monitoring, and evaluating the plan. Ultimately, however, a successful implementation will depend on the enthusiasm and commitment of each member of the Library staff, including our student assistants. Generating and sustaining this commitment will be a key responsibility of Library leadership as this plan unfolds.

Performance Results

Performance results are included under each thrust as part of the Strategic Goals statements in Section 2.

194 - Documents - (10+ Pages)

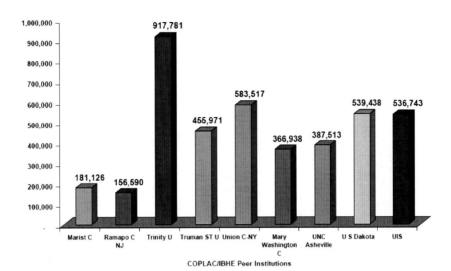

APPENDIX A
Figure 1
Volumes in Library 2004

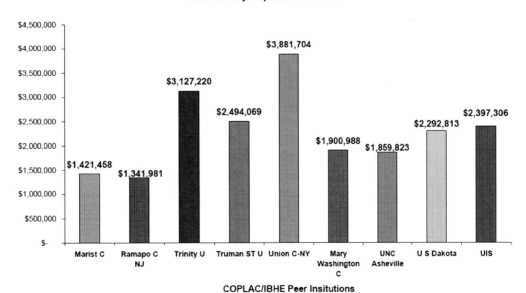

APPENDIX A
Figure 2
Total Library Expenditures 2004

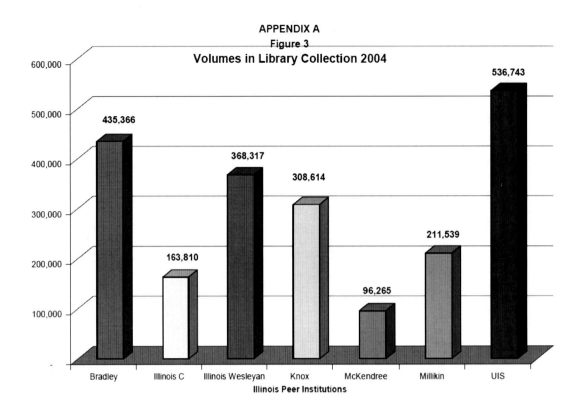

APPENDIX A
Figure 3
Volumes in Library Collection 2004

Illinois Peer Institutions

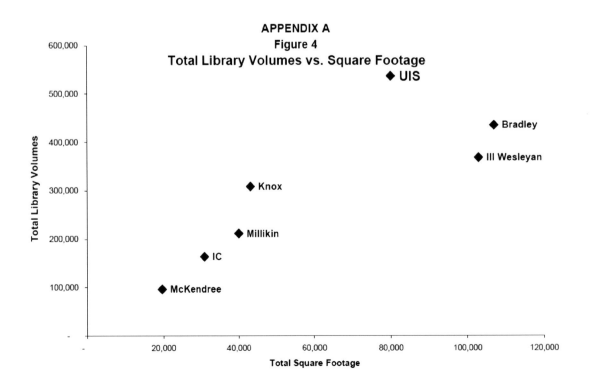

APPENDIX A
Figure 4
Total Library Volumes vs. Square Footage

Total Library Volumes

Total Square Footage

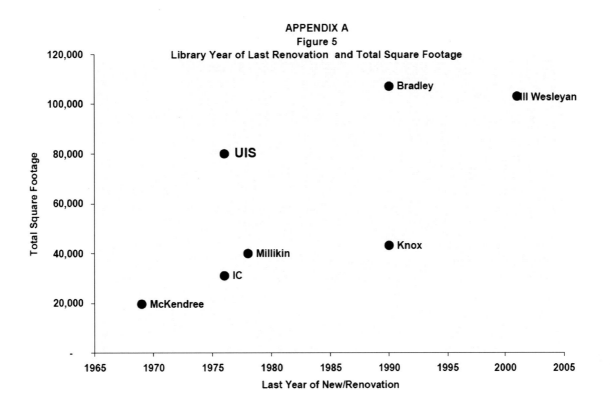

APPENDIX A
Figure 5
Library Year of Last Renovation and Total Square Footage

University of Illinois at Springfield

Appendix B

ACRL STATISTICS QUESTIONNAIRE, 2003-04

Definitions of statistical categories can be found in NISO Z39.7-2004, Information Services and Use: Metrics and statistics for libraries and information providers—Data Dictionary http://www.niso.org/emetrics/current/index.html.

Volumes in Library. Use the ANSI/NISO Z39.7-2004 definition for **volume** as follows:
> *a single physical unit of any printed, typewritten, handwritten, mimeographed or processed work, distinguished from other units by a separate binding, encasement, portfolio, or other clear distinction, which has been cataloged, classified, and made ready for use, and which is typically the unit used to charge circulation transactions. Either a serial volume is bound, or it comprises the serial issues that would be bound together if the library bound all serials.*

Expenditures. Report all expenditures of funds that come to the library from the regular institutional budget, and from sources such as research grants, special projects, gifts and endowments, and fees for service.

Appendix C

Brookens Library Strategic Planning Team
2006

Kim Armstrong, Instructional Services Librarian
Julie Chapman, Instructional Services Librarian
Joan Cormier, Library Technical Assistant
Mollie Freier, Instructional Services Librarian
Denise Green, Instructional Services Librarian
Carole Rahn, Assistant to the Dean
Kathleen Roegge, Library Access Services Manager
Marcia Rossi, Administrative Secretary
Pamela Salela, Instructional Services Librarian
Stephen Smith, Director of Bibliographic Services
Jane Treadwell, University Librarian and Dean of Library Instructional Services
Albert Whittenberg, Associate Director of Educational Technology
Tom Wood, University Archivist

Ryan Becker, UIS Student/Library Access Services Student Assistant